Anonymous

Brahmins and pariahs

An appeal by the indigo manufacturers of Bengal to the British government

Anonymous

Brahmins and pariahs
An appeal by the indigo manufacturers of Bengal to the British government

ISBN/EAN: 9783337150914

Printed in Europe, USA, Canada, Australia, Japan

Cover: Foto ©Andreas Hilbeck / pixelio.de

More available books at **www.hansebooks.com**

͏MINS AND PARIAHS.

AN APPEAL

BY THE

𝔍𝔫𝔡𝔦𝔤𝔬 𝔐𝔞𝔫𝔲𝔣𝔞𝔠𝔱𝔲𝔯𝔢𝔯𝔰 𝔬𝔣 𝔅𝔢𝔫𝔤𝔞𝔩

TO THE

BRITISH GOVERNMENT, PARLIAMENT, AND PEOPLE,

FOR

PROTECTION

AGAINST THE

LIEUT.-GOVERNOR OF BENGAL;

SETTING FORTH THE PROCEEDINGS BY WHICH THIS HIGH OFFICER
HAS INTERFERED WITH THE FREE COURSE OF JUSTICE, HAS
DESTROYED CAPITAL AND TRADE OF BRITISH SETTLERS IN
INDIA, AND HAS CREATED THE PRESENT DISASTROUS CON-
DITION OF INCENDIARISM AND INSURRECTION NOW SPREADING
IN THE RURAL DISTRICTS OF BENGAL.

---

*" Every office in the country is held by men pledged to oppose the settlement of
Europeans in the country, and they are able to make their own statements."*—Letter
from " The Times Calcutta Correspondent," dated from Calcutta, 8th December,
1860, and published in the Times of 14th January, 1861.

LONDON:

JAMES RIDGWAY, 169, PICCADILLY, W.

1861.

BRAHMINS AND PARIAHS.

CHAPTER I.

A CONTRAST.

Two of the principal staples which India produces for exportation are opium and indigo.

In one respect, and in one respect only, opium and indigo resemble each other. They are both cultivated by " a system of advances, which presents some features absolutely identical."[*]

In all other respects these vegetable products can only be compared to be contrasted.

Opium is a drug which is grown for traffic with China, and is that " foreign medicine" which now passes through the Chinese custom houses at a settled duty ; indigo is a harmless dye, which is very welcome at Manchester, and exercises only beneficial effects upon our relations with the rest of the world. Opium is the result of " a system of poppy cultivation under a Government monopoly."[†] Indigo is produced by independent " British settlers, in whose future increase lies the only permanent prosperity of British India."[‡] Opium is produced under a coercive

---

[*] Report of Indigo Commission of 1860, par. 14.
[†] Idem.
[‡] Opinions of Lord William Bentinck and Lord Metcalfe, quoted and adopted in the Report of the Colonization Committee, 1859.

A 2

system which is of such an unrelaxing character that the remuneration to the Ryot has in a quarter of a century scarcely varied, while the remuneration for indigo has kept pace with the increased value of labour, which it has itself tended to create, and is now three times the amount which it was thirty-five years ago.* Indigo has cleared the jungle and turned the wilderness into corn-fields, and the lair of the wild beast into villages; while opium has only covered rich arable lands with poppies, and fixed a system of forced labour akin to slavery upon the people.

In other respects the contrast is still more remarkable. Opium has always been the object of the most tender care to the Government, while the manufacture of indigo has always been a thing to be discouraged, and, if possible, destroyed.† The system by which opium has been produced has always been veiled from the public eye and excluded from all public inquiries; while the system by which indigo is produced has always been made to bear the onus of every passing disturbance, and has been, as State Papers now prove, industriously calumniated by the agents of the governing Company.‡ The obligation of the Ryots to cultivate opium has been enforced by remedies so summary and by punishments so stringent, that neglect or opposition is almost unheard of; while the contracts to cultivate indigo have been denuded of all practical legal remedy, and the planter has been, in this respect, a mere outlaw, left to right himself or to suffer wrong, watched

---

* In 1825 the Ryot received a rupee for twelve bundles of indigo plants, then it rose to a rupee for ten bundles, then to eight and to six. It is now at four bundles the rupee; and as the price of labour increases, the price of the plant will still further rise.

† Evidence of Mr. C. Hollings, Indigo Commissioner, 1860. Evidence.

‡ Report of Indigo Commission, 1860.

by a police which, as the late Lieutenant-Governor of Bengal complains,* are the most corrupt body of officials which the world has ever seen, and at the mercy of the Bengal secretariat, whose policy has ever been to harass and oppress those who, in the language of the covenanted servants of the Company, were " interlopers" in India.†

Opium is popular in the public offices of Calcutta ; and to any suggestion of the grinding slavery it fastens upon the Ryot, the present Lieut.-Governor of Bengal would doubtless reply by some phrase of contempt, such as those he has recently addressed to the indigo planters, or by some bold flight of the imagination, such as those which make up the last Minute he has published. Indigo, on the other hand, after fifty years struggle against the officers of the Civil Service when in its plenitude of power, seems to be at last upon the verge of extinction. In the present Lieut.-Governor of Bengal, the Honourable John Peter Grant, it has found an enemy who unites those qualities in his public functions which are necessary to destroy the constant object of the hostility of the Secretariat of Bengal. At this man's will, and as would appear to us, for no other object than to satisfy the instincts of a traditional hatred,‡ eight millions of

---

* Sir F. Halliday's Minute on the Police.

† See Minute upon the Complaint of the Bengal Indigo Planters' Association *passim*.

‡ "2692. Mr. CAMPBELL.] What may be the annual value of the indigo produced in India ?—The value of the indigo produced in Bengal and the Upper Provinces may be from £2,000,000 to £3,000,000 per annum, varying with the extent of the crops and the market price of the article.

"2693. Is that all produced by English capital and skill, and enterprise ? Nineteen-twentieths of it is produced by British capital and skill.

"2694. You have stated that the annual value of indigo produced is from £2,000,000 to £3,000,000 : what may be the value of the proper-

British capital are to be destroyed ; an annual trade of
£2,000,000 is to cease out of India ; a population of at
least a million native labourers are to be cast out of employ ; * and the whole class of planters, who are now re-
claiming the wilderness, civilizing the people, curing the
sick, relieving the starving, upholding the falling, and
accustoming the suspicious native to associate all these
blessings with employment under an European—all this
class is to be ruined and driven forth, while Mr. J. P.
Grant, like a Russian general superintending the depor-
tation of Tartars from the Crimea, affects to weep over
the ruins and to deplore the necessity.

This is, in a few words, the complaint which the planters of Bengal make to their countrymen in England.
The present Lieut.-Governor of Bengal has sent forth
the word for their annihilation.   In a country where
capital is so scarce that every payment must always be
made beforehand —in a country where Government is a
despotism, and the native looks upon the ruler for the
moment as supreme and irresistible,—the Lieut.-Governor
has caused the people to understand, that in all matters
connected with the growth of indigo he will abide by the
Ryots, and will hold them harmless against the planter ;

ties producing this indigo, and do they belong entirely to English capitalists ? — The value of the properties, including the putnees, talooks,
and zemindaries throughout India, may be from £7,000,000 to
£8,000,000, varying with the value of money and price of indigo, and
entirely held by English settlers and capitalists.

" 2695. Has this capital and property been acquired by men who have
gone to India with nothing but that capital which a European carries
everywhere, namely, perseverance, industry, and skill ?—Yes.—*Evidence
of Mr. J. P. Wise, Colonization Committee,* 2nd *Report,* p. 41.

* In the ploughing season of 1859, before the interference of the
present Lieut.-Governor, the indigo factories of R. Watson and Co. had
17,000 ploughs at work, and upwards of 100,000 men engaged in the
cultivation and manufactures incident to their concerns. This is the
return of one firm alone.

that when his own magistrates shall decide in favour of the planter, he will set aside their decisions; and that even Acts of Council shall be to him no impediment to the pursuit of his own policy, for that he will cause his magistrates to give them what interpretation he may please. In a country where there is no law to compel the observance of a multitude of small indigo contracts; where the native courts are costly, dilatory, and corrupt, and the police are admitted, even by their employers, to be an organized gang of extortioners; where the planter can rely only upon his moral influence for obtaining his own, and the subtle Hindoo and more crafty Mussulman who have pocketed the price of their labour, are eager to seize any excuse for avoiding their obligations;—in such a country, and in such a condition of circumstances as these, the Lieut.-Governor causes, or wilfully suffers the belief to go forth, that Government is desirous that the cultivation of indigo shall cease.* When the natural result happens, and his victims complain, Mr. Grant replies with sneers and by insolent reference to the publicly disproved slanders which were cast upon a former gene-

* In dealing with their own opium ryots, the Government has been very careful to avoid the course which they have adopted with the indigo ryots. So far from exciting them by proclamations, they have ever sedulously refrained from any enquiry as to their grievances. When the opium ryots murmured and almost rebelled, Mr. Farquharson did not issue Commissions or indite Perwannahs. He reported: "I am averse to call for general information from the Districts without absolute necessity. There is no keeping such calls secret, and their spread always does harm in exciting hope or encouraging vain expectation. There can be no doubt in the mind of any one of the fact my simple statement conveys, every sort of country produce being now nearly double what it was three years ago, and labour proportionately high."

A very trifling increase was given, and the rising storm was hushed. This was how the discontents of the opium ryots were met. We shall see, presently, how Mr. Grant interfered, not to quench, but to fan into flame a similar smouldering discontent among the indigo ryots.

ration of planters; and when he is charged with absolute
ignorance of the industry with which he is mischievously
meddling, he replies that he knows the subject well, and
that his knowledge is derived from having, *twenty-five
years ago*, digested a series of *ex parte* charges made by
the civilians against the planters.*

This great public officer has produced an effect which
cannot be comprehended in England. If an English
minister could be found so insane as to declare that
debtors had much to complain of in the obduracy of their
creditors, and that the law ought not to give facilities to
make labourers complete contracts for which they have
received the stipulated remuneration, such a declaration
would cause a very modified mischief. The minister
would disappear before the indignation of the public, and
the debtors and repudiating labourers would soon come
to learn that the law is stronger than the word of the
minister. But in India there are no courts that can meet
these cases in the Mofussil, and Mr. Grant has laboured
that there shall be none. Mr. Grant's hint was taken
all over the country. The Ryots firmly believe that Go-
verment is averse to indigo cultivation, and will support
them in the repudiation of their contracts. An extensive
jaquerie has been the consequence. The Ryots arose
tumultuously, and not only refused to sow indigo, but,

* See Minute upon the Complaint of the Indigo Planters' Association, par. 14.   Mr. Grant says—" I remember saying that I had never
had any experience in an indigo district; and I have no doubt that I
disclaimed all knowledge on the subject of indigo from personal observation.   But I am sure that I did not say that I had no knowledge on
the subject derived from others.   I knew perfectly well native opinion
on the subject; and I had had a peculiar opportunity of becoming
more fully acquainted than most public servants with the common
abuses in connexion with indigo, in all districts, so far back as in 1835,
when I was employed in digesting a mass of reports from every indigo
district in Bengal."

persuaded that they had the Government at their back,
attacked the planters. It has always been found easy to
arouse debtors against creditors, whether at Rome, where
the plebeians were always ready to wipe off their scores
with the patricians; or in England, where not much
rhetoric was necessary to persuade an assault upon the
Jews; or at Hobra, where the Mahometan Ryots felt no
great distaste to attack the house of the one European
who lived among them, to cancel their obligations to
him, and to plunder his property. Alarmed at the
rising against Europeans which this Lieut.-Governor
had produced, the Government sent soldiers into the
districts, which, even during the mutinies, had remained
in unbroken tranquillity, and the Legislative Council
of India passed a law to give, for six months, a summary
remedy in case of breaches of contract. The Lieut.-
Governor again interfered to prevent the action of this
law. He appointed magistrates to carry it out who
were of his own bias; and when even these magistrates,
in the presence of the danger, and impressed by the circumstances which surrounded them, passed sentences
upon the ringleaders of this social revolution, he interfered with the course of justice, revoked the sentences of
his own magistrates, and released the convicted offenders.
Prompt ruin has followed this conduct. Thus protected,
of course the Ryots will not sow, and they will not per-
mit others to sow, and they will destroy all that has been
sown. They have been taught their power of resistance.
They have learned from Mr. Grant how to repudiate
their contracts to sow indigo. That they should have
stopped here would have been contrary to human nature,
or, at least, such natures as we are dealing with. They
are now acquiring of themselves the knowledge of the

difficulty of recovering rents. The last news is, that they are refusing to pay rents to the factory holders even for the rice lands they hold under them. And this wise act of throwing all the rural districts of Bengal into confusion is taken by the Government at a time when we are introducing new taxes, and when the Government officials are making overtures to the country gentlemen of India, to the indigo planters dwelling in the Mofussil, to aid them—for without their aid it can never be done—in the assessment of the income tax. Meanwhile Mr. J. P. Grant looks on with a pleasant chuckle, gently impels the whole class of "interlopers" towards the inevitable precipice, sees with the eye of hope the re-installation of his class in its old exclusiveness of power and supremacy, and pharisaically deplores the necessity of destroying so beneficial a body of traders.

This is the charge which, before the people of England, we bring against the Honourable John Peter Grant, and which we ask the Ministry, the Houses of Parliament, and the Country, to entertain and inquire into.

We are now to prove these allegations.

It will be necessary, for this purpose, to inform the public mind upon many matters with which it is not familiar, and to make our countrymen feel, if possible, some touch of the social atmosphere of our Eastern empire. To pile together mere facts and figures without arrangement or illustration, would only be to produce a statement of intolerable tediousness, which few would read, and by which no one, who does not already know India, could be instructed. We will attempt, by dividing our subject into headings, to lead the reader more easily up, step by step, to the height from which he may overlook the whole iniquity.

CHAPTER II.

THE COVENANTED SERVANT AND THE " INTERLOPER."

It is very difficult for any Englishman to quite realize to himself what a covenanted servant was, and, indeed, still is, in India. We insist upon taking our notion of these men from what we see of them in this country. We adopt the nabob in " Gilbert Gurney," with his indolence and ductility, and his pet rattlesnakes, as a type of the class ; or we fix in our memory some club bore, whose irritable temper and imperious manner to the servants make the room which he chooses to infest uninhabitable to the quiet members of the club. Or we imagine a testy old gentleman wrapped up in flannel, in a house in Baker Street, and scolding a trembling but expectant half-score of nephews and nieces. But with notions like these in our heads we shall never arrive at an understanding of this indigo question. It has, we believe, happened that a retired civilian was rather cut among his English acquaintances because he had boasted proudly that he had been " a collector" in the East. His ignorant friends imagined, that instead of having been a despotic and practically irresponsible sovereign over a country larger than England, he had gone about with a book and an ink-bottle collecting dues from door to door. We must, however, have a better idea than this of the " pucka civilian" before we can have the least inkling of any Eastern question. The worn and decrepit

invalid whom we see about London is no more like the
Civil servant of the East, in his pride and in his power,
than is the lion of the forests of the Atlas, reposing in
his strength, or crushing in his spring, like the harmless,
and rather mangy beast who does duty as the type of
his race in an English menagerie. In the early days of
the Indian empire our civilian went out from England a
mere boy, and he found himself at once a member of a
dominant and privileged class. The millions of Hin-
dustan all bowed themselves to the dust before him. He
was taught—and how soon is such a lesson learnt—to
consider himself a superior being to those around him.
As the common phrase in India runs, he was one of the
heaven-born :* as a recent official report expresses it, he
was one of " the nobility of India." After a few years
of subordinate office, with a salary greater than that of
grey-headed barristers in judicial positions at home, he
became, in some far-away province, the pro-consul of the
great sovereign Company. He had no knowledge of
law, either in its principles or its practice, yet he sat in
judgment on ten millions of mankind, and Indian princes
were his suitors. He knew little, if any thing, of the
principles of finance, yet he administered the finances as
well as the judicial functions of his province. He was
ignorant of the habits and customs of the people, and he
had a bare smattering of their language, yet his fiat was
practically without appeal in all cases, from a contest
between two farmers to the confiscation of the possessions
of an ancient line of princes. He was irresponsible. No

---

* This term should have been "heaven-taught," for, as we learn from
old letters, it was adopted in sneering allusion to the facility with which
civilians passed from the functions of clerks to those of judges, governors,
legislators, and financiers, without any special education for any of these
duties. The system, however, is now in a transition state.

crime, however great, could ever be proved against him.
In the history of the Company there is scarcely an instance of a " senior merchant," or a " collector," having
been publicly or privately dismissed the service. If he
failed to make satisfactory financial returns he was removed to a less lucrative province, but this was the only
crime known to the Company. If he provoked an expensive insurrection he was censured; but mere acts of
despotism followed by no pecuniary loss to the Company
had no guilt in their eyes. The press was gagged; there
was no European public opinion; the echoes of great
atrocities waxed faint, as they came across the ocean
and vaguely fell upon the ears of Englishmen at home :
he was a great despot for good or for bad as the case
might happen. There was a general notion here that
the returned " nabob's " life had been a series of crimes
and horrors, but no one ever knew any particulars. Lord
Clive, whose most conspicuous civil quality was the disgust with which he looked upon the corruption by which
he was surrounded, was called " the wicked Lord Clive;"
other less famous old Indians also had their evil reputa-
tions; but the mere " senior merchant" or " collector"
was safe in his insignificance when he had reached this
country—a Verres of this degree was too obscure to call
forth a Cicero.

To tell how this power was abused is unnecessary.
As a rule, such absolute power never yet was obtained
without being abused. Exceptions there doubtless were
of honourable men, who, so far as their imperfect information enabled them to do so, used their tremendous
power only to do what they believed to be justice. India
is even now filled with traditions of enormities which,
seen through the medium of great distance, are remem-

bered only in a ludicrous sense, the wickedness being
sunk in the absurdity. Those "nabobs" were but too
often extortionate governors and corrupt judges. They
shook the pagoda tree as violently as they could, and
they made haste to become rich and to quit the country.
But they were "the nobility of India." The natives,
from the Nawab to the Coolie, were in the language of
those days "niggers:" the king's army, and even the
king's judges, were an inferior class to themselves ;* but
the few straggling settlers who had found their way from
England without being decorated with the Company's
covenant were very far beneath the "niggers." They
were Pariahs, the lowest of the low.

Why do we go back to those days anterior to 1814?
Not, certainly, to fasten the crimes of those early tyrants
upon the civilians of the present day. We would not
disgrace ourselves or our cause by following the example
of our Lieut.-Governor, who in his apology, insinuates
what he dares not assert, by taunting the planters in a
sneering way with the disturbances which sometimes
happened in a former generation, but which, as his own
Commissioners have shewn, have very long since been
obsolete.† Nor do we seek to cast any suspicion upon

---

* It is only within a few weeks that the Judges of the Supreme
Court have been obliged to protest in their places against the insolent
and contemptuous terms applied to them by Mr. Eden before the Indigo
Commission.

† "There are," says Mr. Grant in his Minute, "no affrays, no forci-
ble entries, and unlawful carrying off of crops and cattle, no ploughing
up of other men's lands, no destruction of trees and houses, no unlawful flogging and confinement in godowns, now reported. Even the
offence of kidnapping Ryots seems almost arrested."
Now let us contrast this with the report of Mr. Grant's own Secretary, who, looking back for thirty years to recapitulate all the rural
crimes that have happened among 20,000,000 of people, drew that
"Report of the Indigo Commission" which has just reached England.

the Civil service, *as a body*, that they are actuated by any sordid views, or by any worse motives than those of

Mr. Seton Karr and a Missionary, and another Civil servant, and a native, thus report upon these calumnies (pars. 85 to 88) :—

"Of actual destruction of human life, comparatively few cases of late years have been brought to our knowledge, as proved ; and we have no wish to lay great stress on a list of *forty-nine serious cases* which are shewn to have occurred over a period of *thirty years* in different parts of the country, because violent affrays, ending in homicide or wounding, are, we are happy to say, of *not nearly such frequent occurrence as they used to be; and affrays are not peculiar to indigo planting. They occur equally where the plant is not grown.*

"From the returns supplied by the magistrates of some of the most important districts for the last five years, some of which are entirely blank, it is quite clear that investigations into those fights *between the adherents of Zemindar* [not Ryot] *and planter,* which used to carry desolation, terror, and demoralization into a dozen villages at a time, no longer disfigure our criminal annals to the extent they used to do. Even in Nuddea, as will be seen from the return, the cases were few *in the years preceding* 1859 *and* 1860." [When Mr. Grant's proclamations began to excite the populace.] "Some of this good result is, no doubt, due to the working of Act IV. of 1840, for giving summary possession of lands ; to the law for the exaction of recognizances and security against apprehended breaches of the peace, namely Act V. of 1848; and to the establishment of subdivisions with convenient circles of jurisdiction. A good deal is owing also to the acquisition by planters of rights in lands, and to the peace and quiet which usually follow such acquisition, as far as affrays and fights are concerned; but something also is due to the better skill and management of factories generally, and, we doubt not, to the good sense and good feeling of the most influential planters.

"Affrays carried out with premeditation, on a large scale, by means of hired clubmen, we are thus happy to pronounce *rare in some districts, and in others unknown.*

"Then, as to the burning of bazaars and houses, we have a clear admission from a gentleman whose character entitles him to great respect (A. 670), that he 'has known of such acts ;' but no well-proved instance of this sort has been brought to our notice in any oral evidence. In one or two instances mentioned to us, when a fire took place, it was a matter of doubt whether its origin was not accidental ; and we cannot, therefore, but acquit the planters, as a body, of any practice of the sort, though we do not mean to say that cases of arson do not occur in Lower Bengal, in consequence of indigo disputes. A crime of this kind would, from its very openness, attract attention, and should be susceptible of the clearest proof."

After finding that only one case of "knocking down houses" had

prejudice, and class-arrogance; but we are trying to make the English public understand the traditional antagonism of the Civil Service to all European settlers, and we must, for that purpose, refer to the Civil servant as he was when the Company was absolute.

It is easy to comprehend how a despot of this kind, whether using his power for good or for ill, would detest the appearance of an European in his kingdom. In effect, nothing was more dreaded, either by civilian or by the Company. The records of early days have now been published, and they are full of the anxiety of the Civil Service to keep European eyes and ears far away from them. In 1775, Mr. Francis declared, in a formal Minute, "that Europeans in Bengal, beyond the number the services of Government required, are an useless weight and embarrassment to the Government, and an injury to the country, and that they are people to whom no encouragement should be given." In 1792 the Company assured Lord Cornwallis that the licenses to go to India should "not exceed five or six, or, at the utmost, ten" every year. In 1818, "John Jebb and James Pattison, Esquires," on the part of the Company, made an elaborate remonstrance to Mr. Canning against the

been brought forward, and that that had been taken into court, and the sentence of the magistrate reversed in the Sudder in favour of the planters, the report proceeds—

" As to outrages on women, which, more than any other act, might offend the prejudice and arouse the vindictiveness of a people notoriously sensitive as to the honour of their families, we are happy to declare that our most rigid inquiries could bring to light only one case of the kind. And when we came to examine into its foundation, so seriously affecting the character of one planter, and, through him, the body of the planters in a whole district, or as affording any clue to the excitement of the past season, we discovered that there were very reasonable grounds for supposing that no outrage on the person of the woman had ever taken place."

grant by the Government of licenses to go to India, and, among other grievances arising from these licenses, these gentlemen complain that " among the British residents in India, there is a strong disposition to assert *what they conceive to be* their constitutional and indefeasible rights, a general leaning towards each other, and a common jealousy of the authority of Government."

Strange to say, this remonstrance was lost upon Mr. Canning, who answered that Parliament, when it gave the Board of Control power to grant these licenses, " was led to apprehend the existence in the Court of Directors of a disposition in respect of the granting of these permissions the very reverse of facility and profusion."

It was in vain that men of statesmanlike minds attempted to overcome the small trading views of the Company, and to overrule the objections of the distant proconsuls ; in vain that Sir Charles Metcalfe, in 1829, minuted that " he had long lamented that our countrymen in India were excluded from the possession of land and other ordinary rights of peaceable subjects ;"* and further that " he was convinced that our possession of India must always be precarious unless we take root by having an influential portion of the population attached to our Government by common interests and sympathies." It was in vain, also, that Lord William Bentinck, in a Minute of three months' later date, said, " The sentiments expressed by Sir Charles Metcalfe have my entire concurrence."† The Company continued to oppose all coloni-

* To see this terror of " interlopers" fully pourtrayed, the reader should refer to a volume published by Messrs. Thacker, Spink, and Co., of Calcutta (1854), under the title of " Papers relating to the Settlement of Europeans in India," where all the correspondence cited above is set forth.

† " Papers relating to Settlement of Europeans in India," p. 39. We cannot afford to omit the testimony of this great Governor-General to

zation in India, using this word "colonization" as a pre-
posterous figment, as they did indeed to the last, and as

the usefulness of the planters, even in that early day, and to their general
innocence of the charges calumniously brought against them by the
Company and its servants.   It occurs in the same Minute quoted above.
Lord William Bentinck says—

"It has been supposed that many of the indigo planters, resident in
the interior, have misconducted themselves, acting oppressively towards
the natives, and with violence and outrage towards each other.   Had
the case been so, I must still have thought it just to make large allow-
ances for the peculiar position in which they stood.   They have been
denied permission to hold lands in their own names.   They have been
driven to evasion, which has rendered it difficult for them to establish
their just claims by legal means, as they have had to procure the plant
required by them through a system of advances, which, in all branches
of trade, is known to occasion much embarrassment, and to lead to much
fraud.   They have possessed no sufficient means of preventing the
encroachment of rival establishments, still less of recovering their dues
from needy and improvident Ryots.   Further, we must not forget that
the restrictions imposed upon the resort of Europeans to this country
have operated to compel the houses of business often to employ persons
in the management of their concerns in the interior whom they would
not have employed if they had had a wider scope of choice.   It would
not be wonderful if abuses should be found to have prevailed under such
circumstances, or if the weakness of the law should have sometimes led
to violence in the assertion of real or supposed rights.   But under all the
above circumstances of disadvantages, the result of my inquiries is, a
firm persuasion (contrary to the conclusions I had previously been disposed to draw) that the occasional misconduct of the planters is as
nothing when contrasted with the sum of good they have diffused around
them.   In this, as in other cases, the exceptions have so attracted attention, as to be mistaken for a fair index of the general course of things.
Breaches of the peace being necessarily brought to public notice, the
individual instances of misconduct appear under the most aggravated
colours; but the numerous nameless acts, by which the prudent and
orderly, while quietly pursuing their own interests, have contributed to
the national wealth, and to the comfort of those around them, are
unnoticed or unknown.   I am assured that much of the agricultural
improvement which many of our districts exhibit, may be directly
traced to the indigo planters therein settled; and that, as a general truth,
it may be stated (with the exceptions which in all general truths
require to be made), that every factory is, in its degree, the centre of a
circle of improvement, raising the persons employed in it and the
inhabitants of the immediate vicinity, above the general level.   The
benefit in the individual cases may not be considerable, but it seems to
be sufficient to shew what might be hoped from a more liberal and en-
lightened system."

the Civil Service does now. As to the Civil servants, no English squire ever looked with more disgust upon a notorious poacher walking through the preserves, his audacity legalized by a footpath, than did a "Civil servant" upon an "uncovenanted European" coming into the Mofussil protected by his license. He was a new power. Not very formidable, indeed, was this poor interloper to the great aggregate mammon-worshipper, or to the despotic master of the surrounding population. In those early days he was only there by sufferance of the Government at Calcutta, for he could not go eleven miles from Calcutta for pleasure or business without a passport; his license might at any time be withdrawn, and himself deported to England, because he had "incurred the displeasure of the Government," without further reason assigned. While dwelling in the Mofussil he was obliged to bribe the police annually to give him a character, and his only security was to keep as quiet as possible. But still he was to the "Civilian" a symbol of freedom, of criticism, and even of publicity. He always suspected in him "a strong disposition to assert what he must conceive to be his constitutional and indefeasible rights," and, even worse still, to tell the princes and peasants around of their rights. As time grew on, our civilian found himself under the eye of a man not so easily removable as before, who, when he was corrupt, could penetrate the corruption of his acts, and who, although he was certain not to be believed at Calcutta, would make a noise about them. Later still, when practically the planter could no longer be deported in a Company's ship, the "interloper" was found telling the natives that it was no part of their duty to find the collector gratis with bearers and refreshments when he

B 2

passed through their villages, like a monarch on a progress; and the Ryots round the indigo factory were even encouraged to tell the mighty lord that he must pay for his supplies like a common mortal. Mr. Dalrymple, a partner in, and for many years manager of, Messrs. Watson and Co.'s factories, recollects the first instance of this refusal.

It has happened in those more modern days, that a few years after some outrageously unjust sentence in a dispute between a planter and a neighbouring Zemindar, the planter came into the management of the Zemindar's property, acting for his heirs, and found among his papers a bond for a very large sum of money, given by the very judge who had delivered the iniquitous sentence. Both Zemindar and judge are dead, but the bond and the planter are still in existence.

This was the position of the civilian and the interloper in the Mofussil—a traditional state of antagonism. Thus it has been, broken, of course, by individual exceptions, to the present day. Even that eminent "pucka civilian," Mr. Hawkins, who has run the whole course of Indian offices, and has been magistrate, judge, collector, session-judge, commissioner of excise and revenue, and lastly, a Judge of the Sudder Dewanny Adawlut—even that eminent covenanted servant, in his evidence before the "Colonization of India Committee, 1858," acknowledges and regrets the estrangement of the settlers and the Company's officers, and attempts to account in a mild official way for the false opinions which each class has of the other. "I believe," he says, "that the indigo planters and the Civil servants do take a view of each other, which is perhaps forced upon them from the positions which they occupy, which is very unfortunate. The indigo planter

very often lives at a distance from the station, and is never
heard of except he appears in court for doing something
contrary to law; and the judge gets the idea that every
indigo planter is an obstreperous gentleman. The indigo
planter hears of the judge, not as the judge actually is,
but as his agent reports him to the indigo planter, and he
very often imposes upon both; he imposes upon the indigo planter, and gives as his reason for the dismissal of a
case in court that the judge had acted unjustly, or that
the judge did so and so, or that he wanted so and so;
they are both represented to each other in false lights.
But this kind of thing is forced upon us by the difficulties
of our position."

Mr. Hawkins denies that the Company's officers have
any prejudice against this " obstreperous gentleman," and
he is so condescending as to admit, in opposition to what
Calcutta believes to be the declared opinion of Mr. J. P.
Grant, that " he has known a number of indigo planters
who are perfect gentlemen, fit associates for anybody."
He says, also, that of the grievances of the planters,
" the chief is the police system, and the system of judicial
administration,* to which the settlers say they object."

---

* " 2654. Have you individually suffered from the consequences of
administration such as you have described?—I have seriously suffered;
and by way of illustrating the working of the system, I may proceed to
narrate a few instances. In the year 1833-4 the estate of Buldakal, in
the Tipperah district, was put up for sale for arrears of revenue. I
became the purchaser, and deposited the amount required by the law in
bank notes and Company's paper, pending the commissioner of revenue's approval of the sale ; and on that officer's doing so, I paid into
the Treasury of Commillah the whole amount, 1,15,000 rupees, and
received the collector's order to take possession of the estate. I may
observe, at that time the law permitting Europeans to hold lands in India
had not been promulgated, but it had passed all the preliminary stages,
so I was obliged to get the permission of Government in anticipation
to hold the estate : this was immediately granted by Sir Charles Metcalfe, then Lieutenant-Governor of Bengal. The ex-Zemindar appealed

That is to say, the judge's police persecute him, and extort from him, and his court affords him no remedy ; yet the judge is not the enemy of the planter! The feeling of the Civil Service of India, with regard to the settler, is apparent in this, that an eminent civilian, one of the best and most liberal-minded of his class, speaks of it as no special discouragement to British settlers, that they should live under the pest of a set of protected native extortioners, and that they should be practically outlawed in

to the Board of Revenue against the sale, and the Board had the power to reverse it upon any legal grounds : the petition was sent by the Board back to the commissioner for his opinion, and that commissioner was not the same who had previously upheld the sale, but the collector of Chittagong, temporarily put in charge of the commissioner's office, and he recommended the reversal of the sale, upon grounds utterly unfounded, and in contravention of the law. First, he said the estate had been sold without making it known that the subordinate tenures had lapsed : this was not required, as the Permanent Settlement Laws of 1793 declare this; and every tenant knows it, and one instance of such a notice before a sale could not be shewn. Secondly, because the petition stated the estate had been sold at or towards sunset : this was purely false, as the sale took place in open cutcherry, about 12 o'clock. Thirdly, that the collector was a relative of mine, and had favoured me by accepting Company's paper as security for my bid : this, again, was incorrect ; but the acting commissioner did not give himself the trouble of duly inquiring. His thoughts turned upon benefiting the Government, for he reported that it would be fair to the under tenants to give greater publicity : and that, as the estate was a very valuable one, he would, in recommending the reversal of this sale, advise the purchase of it on behalf of Government at the next sale. The Board adopted the recommendation, and illegally dispossessed me of a valuable property, and purchased it on the next sale-day, and that estate is now held by Government.

" 2655. Sir *Erskine Perry.*] What did they purchase it at ?—Merely the difference of the increased revenue up to the date of sale.

" 2656. *Chairman.*] Have you suffered in any other case besides that which you have mentioned ?—I have suffered, in connexion with other matters in several ways. * * * Europeans of education and character have not been encouraged to take the appointments of deputy magistrates; natives of family, and fortune, and respectability, have not been selected, but worn-out darogahs, of doubtful reputation, and others physically unfit, have been chosen for these most important situations."
—*Evidence of Mr. M'Nair.*

all civil cases.   Mr. Hawkins cannot help dropping into the track of thought in which his ideas have flowed all his life.   He is too wise to say, " The network of corruption is good enough for the nigger, and what is good enough for the nigger is good enough for these settlers;" and perhaps he does not acknowledge to himself that he thinks so, but this peeps out as the active spirit of his evidence.

One authenticated anecdote is better than a thousand general propositions, but unfortunately we cannot expand our proofs, as the Colonization Committee has done, into four folio volumes.   We must again throw into a foot-note Mr. Dalrymple's account of his dealings with the police and with a district magistrate.*

* Mr. J. R. Dalrymple is asked by the Committee—

" 3194. On what grounds, from your experience, do you complain of the state of the police at present?—They are extortionate; they are corrupt in every sense of the word; they extort from all classes, and get up false cases ; they instigate quarrels ; they instigate both the lower orders, over whom they have great power, and also the Zemindars, to quarrel, and principally with Europeans.

" 3195. Have you had personal experience of that extortion and corruption ?—I have.

" 3196. Could you briefly and clearly give us a specimen of such corruption and extortion which you yourself have undergone ?—Yes, in the case of a darogah : he applied to me for allowance, which he said he had been in the habit of receiving from the former proprietor of a concern that we had just purchased.   It was on our taking possession the man came to me for money.   I refused to give it him, and he was dissatisfied.   Shortly afterwards he left the district; but before the manufacturing season commenced, *the most particular time of the whole year for an indigo planter, when the river is rising*, he was re-appointed to the station.   He again applied for the money, and I still refused : we had only worked a few days when he shut the factories, by preventing the people from working.   He came to me in the evening and asked for his money again, and after much consideration, and seeing that the concerns were stopped through his opposition, I gave him a certain sum of money, the sum of £60.   We got on very well till the manufacturing was about closing again, when he demanded the balance of what he said was due to him, and I again positively refused ; *he completely shut the factories, and*

Hearing such cases as these, well might a Committee of the House of Commons wonder at the continued sur-

we did not work another day after that : the plant went all under water, and I had only recourse to a magistrate, 54 miles distant. I went to the magistrate, and he happened to be from home: he was out in the district. It was ten days before I had a hearing. After hearing me, he called for the darogah. The darogah came to the station, accompanied by the working people and small cultivators, and presented a petition as from them against me, accusing me of murder, arson, rape, and every offence that could be committed, and the magistrate took up the case ; but, on allowing me to cross-examine them, they got confused, and said they did not even know what was in the body of their petition, and they acknowledged that the petition had been written by one of the lower officers of the thannah. *For* 18 *months* my case against the darogah for extortion was undecided, and I had several trips to Kishnagur, being called in by the magistrate, and no hearing was given, and the magistrate was shortly after removed ; and a new magistrate came, and he called up the case, and decided it, without giving me any notice or calling for any of the witnesses. *He exculpated the darogah, re-appointed him to another station, and recommended the Government that I should be severely punished for having acknowledged bribing the darogah.* We lost a very large sum from not being able to work off the plant.

" 3197. Was it the original sum of £60 which you gave the darogah, to which the magistrate referred ?—Yes ; that was the money I gave him to allow the workmen to come to the factories : we lost many thousand rupees besides that, in being unable to work off the plant.

" 3198. How was the darogah exculpated ?—Merely that the magistrate disbelieved the statement, and said that I should not have bribed a policeman.

" 3199. On what ground did the magistrate find you guilty of bribing the darogah ?—On my own acknowledgment that I had given him the £60. I made a statement of the whole of the facts as they took place.

" 3200. Supposing you had not given the £60, what loss would you probably have incurred ?—We lost about £2000 eventually.

" 3201. What would have been the loss if you had not paid that £60 ? —About £6000.

" 3202. Mr. *W. Vansittart.*] In fact you bribed the darogah exactly one year's salary : they get 50 rupees a month ?—No, they got 30 rupees at that time.

" 3203. Then you gave him two years' salary ?—It may be : I know that he was in the habit of receiving 150 rupees a month from the factories before we purchased them.

" 3204. *Chairman.*] In what year did this happen ?—It is some twenty years ago ; but it is a common thing to this day.

" 3205. Do you give this case as a solitary instance, or as a general

vival of any British capital and industry against such
odds.

" Nothing," say the Committee in their Report, " more
" strongly impresses an inquirer into the foundation and
" progress of our Indian Empire than the contrast which,
" as regards British residence, it presents to our other
" dependencies.   While free settlement, as in the neigh-
" bouring island of Ceylon, has formed the basis of our
" colonial system, and the cause of its prosperity, the
" exclusion of free settlers has marked the origin and the
" progress of our Indian Government. Statesmen, indeed,
" like Lord William Bentinck and Lord Metcalfe, saw, in
" the future increase of British settlers, the only per-
" manent prosperity of British India ; and English, and
" even Indian opinion, has gradually followed in the track
" of those more observant and profounder minds.   Even
" now, although the principle of free settlement has been
" recognised by British legislation, *traces of the old ex-*
" *clusive system are said to linger still.   Though they may*
" *be removed in fact, they are stated to exist in feeling.*
" Thus we are told by a very competent witness, that a
" ' cold shade is thrown over European adventurers in
" India ;' and by another, that a feeling of ' dislike to
" settlers' exists among civilians ; that the civilians, as
" distinguished from the settlers, are ' too much of a
" caste ;' and that the covenanted service is, ' as it were,
" the nobility of India.' "

Such have been the British Brahmins of India and the

specimen of what may occur to a gentleman situated as you have been,
in the part of Bengal with which you are familiar ?— I have known
many such cases.

" 3206.—Up to the present time ?—*Up to the present time.*

" 3207. In the long time you have been in the country have you
marked any improvement in the state of the police ?—No, not generally.

British Pariahs of India, as, after long inquiry, their conditions have been developed by the impartial judgment of a Committee of English gentlemen.

The unceasing effort of the white Brahmin has been to exterminate the white Pariah. In the last century he shut him out from India altogether. When he could no longer keep the door entirely closed against him, he still openly avowed his dislike of him, and placed every impediment to his winning his way into the Mofussil.* When he had made good his position in the Mofussil, the Brahmin ignored him as much as possible, refused him all legal remedies, and surrounded him with Brahmin myrmidons, in the shape of a hungry police, and with native assistant-magistrates, who were, for the most part, promoted policemen. When even these strong measures would not kill this tenacious caste, the white Brahmins proposed to make the existence in India of the objects of their dislike impossible, by subjecting their lives and property to native judges and native juries—they themselves, the white Brahmins, being specially exempted from any such jurisdiction. More recently still, the white Brahmins have proposed to disarm these white Pariahs, and to leave them alone in the wilds of India, without means of defence against any wandering band of robbers, and a temptation to the cupidity of the surrounding natives. When foiled in these malevolent and, indeed, remembering the isolated position of the European, horrible attempts, the white Brahmin caste has at length found an effective instrument for its purpose. The present high-priest of the Civil

* "It appears even now to be doubted by legal authorities whether Europeans can enter, without a license, those parts of India which have been acquired within the present century. Your Committee recommend the removal of this doubt by legislative enactment." (Report of Colonization Committee, 1859.)

Service Juggernaut has revived against the white Pariah the old calumnies which were invented and refuted in years past. He has, whether in ignorance or in prejudice, abused the influence of high official station to ruin the only real English interest grown to adult strength in the plains of Bengal. He has attempted, vainly, as we believe, to poison the minds of the European public against their countrymen. He has succeeded in making the natives discontented, dishonest, and insurgent. He has detorted the streams of justice, and brought Government pressure to bear upon the judgment-seat. He has threatened, dismissed, and promoted magistrates according as they gave him satisfaction by their judgments. He has set his favourites to the work of meddling with the business of the planter, with strong instances before them of promotion given for zeal in similar employment. And while enforcing, with most stringent energy, the special laws which give summary remedies against the Ryot who may refuse to cultivate opium or salt for his masters, he has by his proclamations excited the indigo Ryot to rise against his planter creditor, to ruin his trade, and to destroy the security of his person.

How Mr. John Peter Grant has done this we shall proceed to tell in the following pages.

CHAPTER III.

THE INDIGO PLANTER.

As a general proposition there are no roads in India. It was the policy of the Civil Service, and of the masters of the Civil Service, to keep the land as impenetrable as possible, except to the gatherer of revenue.*

The traveller who, upon elephant-back or horse-back, or carried by bearers, shall travel over the broad flats and wide-spread rice-fields of Bengal, will, from time to time, light upon a comfortable European built house, situated in a pleasant park or a carefully cultivated flower garden. All around it are swarthy villages, half hidden by their invariable belt of trees. There are Mussulmans and

---

* The Colonization Committee, 1859, in their Report, say—"It has been truly said by one of the earliest witnesses examined, that one of the first wants of a settler is facility of access to the interior of the country. The Indian Government, however, held the country the greater part of a century before a main line of road was commenced even through the most populous parts of India. This is a neglect which even those witnesses who have been connected with the Government of India acknowledge and deplore. It was justly considered one of the principal causes of the want of a due supply of cotton from India by the Committee on Cotton Cultivation, presided over by Mr. Bright in 1848. The Grand Trunk Road was not begun before the days of Lord William Bentinck in 1836. It is stated that Mr. Halliday had complained in a Minute to Government of the wretched state of the roads near the seat of government itself. One witness asserts, that at a distance of forty miles from Calcutta there are no roads practicable for carts. It is stated by another witness recently there, that even now a road from Calcutta to Jessore is only just being made. 'Between Calcutta and Dacca,' says Mr. Underhill, 'the bridges are broken down, and the road is in perfect disrepair.' This was so late as the year 1854." We may add, that it is the same at this day.

Hindoos lying about languidly in the shade, and a few children driving bullocks over the plain, or passing to and fro up to the European house. If it be early spring, when the rice is not growing, there is no labour going on;* perhaps a couple of Hindoos may be repairing a broken cart, but, generally speaking, the male population will be squat inside their mud and bamboo huts, or recumbent under the shadow of the trees, and you may advance unimpeded towards the house. That villa is the metropolis of the encircling villages. It is not like the abode of a Hill Rajah or even of a Bengal Zemindar, a half-fortified building with armed retainers about it: it is an open Eastern house, with its verandahs and broad windows, and unclosed doors, something much more unprotected than an English villa. As you approach it, you will probably see European children playing on the greensward, or riding on horses led by syces, watched by their mother from the verandah, and accompanied by native nurses.† There is a crowd issuing from the cut-

* The Ryot never works more than three hours a day upon an average, and generally in the cool of the morning. The weeding of the indigo is chiefly done by the women and children, for it is done at a time when there is no other labour for them.

† Mr. Seton Karr corroborates our statement in his earlier writings. He says, in an article in the *Calcutta Review*, whereof he is the putative parent :—

" We leave it to such as have seen the ins and outs of the Mofussil to descant on the style of life led by a planter at the head of a large concern, with rights long established, and therefore secure, his generous hospitality, his frank and open deportment, his ready reception of the European traveller, his kindness to those Ryots who ask his aid or advice. But there is one feature in his present life on which we dwell with peculiar pleasure, and which we cannot pass over now. Isolated from his fellow-men, and surrounded by those of different colour and creed, the Indian of the " old school," the Indian so easily satirized in by-gone novels and short-lived farces, was seldom without one of those wretched incumbrances which here and there still usurp the place of the wife. The practice once so common even in Calcutta and other

cherry, where the master of the house is sitting in a self-established court of arbitration, and later in the evening you may see a larger crowd of Bonooa women, to whom the European lady is giving advice and medicine, and tending the multiform maladies of their children. It is an Eastern patriarchal scene; but you are convinced, as you look upon it, how utterly impossible it must be for that European to live thus alone—one single English family among thousands of Asiatics—if he had not acquired a moral influence over the natives, and if his presence were not felt to be a benefit to the population.* That any man should commit violence and rapine, and should live thus open and unprotected, with his domestic ties about him, is a self-evident absurdity which no man who has ever been in India can honestly assert, or can otherwise than dishonestly insinuate.

The sustenance of this house, and of all the comforts

large stations naturally ceased there, as soon as unmarried ladies began to "come out" from England, but lingered more tenaciously in out-districts and isolated factories. Its traces are now fainter and fainter; and the planter's home is often adorned by the presence of the pure English wife, and the amiable English daughter, with feelings and tastes as genuine as those of residents in the country at home, and wanting only in the bright glow of English health to make the parallel complete."—*Calcutta Review*, vol. ii. p. 217.

* Mr. Walters, the magistrate of the city of Dacca, who has dwelt with especial severity upon a few instances of bad men in troubled times, some of which will always be found, in any body of men, in his return to the Governor-General's Circular of the 29th December, 1829, says—

"That some of the planters are held in much estimation by the natives; that they are constantly called upon to arbitrate disputes between relatives or neighbours; that they are the frequent dispensers of medicine to the sick, of advice to those in difficulty, of pecuniary aid to those in need, on the occasion of family events, which would otherwise involve them for life with native money-lenders; and that their never-failing acquiescence in the wants and wishes of their poor neighbours has thus tended, in some measure, to exalt the British name and character, I can vouch from my own knowledge of the fact."

that surround it, depend upon the vats and drying-house which lie contiguously to it, like the barns and beast-houses of an English homestead.*

How did all this arise in such an out of the world spot?

It is all the work of one of that despised and hated pariah class of British settlers—that class which all the statesmen of India and of England seek to increase, and which the present Lieutenant-Governor of Bengal is now destroying.†

It is now many years since the present proprietor of

---

* We are careful to advance nothing in this statement which cannot be proved by living testimony, or by state documents.

The Colonization Committee, 1859, in their Report, say—

" It is stated by witnesses generally, that ' wherever Europeans have settled, a marked improvement in the country has followed ;' the various products of the land have been developed. Settlers have taken the lead in introducing steam navigation, and in discovering its indispensable auxiliaries, coal and iron; in the extension of roads, and in generally lowering the cost of production.

" It is justly observed by Mr. Marsham, that from their intercourse with the people, settlers must naturally ' know more what is passing in their minds' than the agents of the Government; the position of the settlers rendering them vigilant and interested observers of the tendency of native opinion.

" Where they reside, the rate of interest, often exorbitantly high, becomes reduced. The circulation of ready money is extended, and a steady rise takes place in the rate of wages.

" Another good effect of settlement is its tendency to promote the maintenance of order. A large extension of the number of settlers over India would be a considerable guarantee against any future insurrection, and would tend to lessen the necessity for maintaining our expensive army."

† When we speak of the hostility of the Civil Service, we mean, of course, that spirit of hostility which actuates the body, and which is manifested conspicuously and disastrously in the acts of the fanatics of the class. We shall see hereafter that many individuals of the caste do not resist the evidence of their senses; and, under Lieut.-Governors other than Mr. Grant, have dared to tell the truth. There is as much difference between civilians like Mr. Hawkins or Sir F. Halliday and Mr. J. P. Grant, as there is between an ordinary Brahmin and a Nana Sahib.

this house and factory, or his predecessor, came alone
into this district, to employ his energy and his capital in
the manufacture of indigo. He was not allowed to buy
or lease land when he came there. There was a native
Zemindar, or feudal land-owner, who held over the land
and the Ryots the same sort of power of indefinite exaction which our old feudal lords held over their villeins.
There was also a judge, who was perhaps, in those days
of corruption, in the Zemindar's pay. The new settler
wanted to buy indigo—that is to have an immediate
necessity for a perishable article. In a hundred days the
crop of indigo is grown, and cut, and manufactured.
When once ripe, it must be cut; when once cut, it must
be carried straight to the vats. It will not keep,—" Le
vin est tiré il faut le boire."

How was he to get the natives to procure him the
vegetable he had come so far and spent so much to obtain
in order to manufacture into dye? ·He soon found that
the whole system of the country was to pay beforehand. The little farmers (Ryots) were, in effect, paupers.
They had no capital. They could not afford to buy the
seed, nor to subsist till the indigo would grow. All their
rice crops were mortgaged over and over again to the
native money-lender, who had made them advances at
from 60 to 100 per cent. interest upon them.

This is the case all over India. Industry insists upon
mortgaging itself to capital. Every artificer works upon
advances, and these advances, when made by the native
usurers, is never at less than 60 per cent.

Our new settler bowed to the custom of the country,
called his neighbours together, and offered them advances
" *without interest*," to give him indigo next season at a
stipulated price. The money was taken eagerly. It

was also necessary to supply seed, and the seed was added at a nominal charge. Perhaps the Ryot was honest, and sowed, perhaps he did not; but we will assume that he did.

At the proper season the vats were ready, and the indigo was ripe for cutting. But now began the planter's difficulty. When he went to cut and carry his indigo there were other claimants on the ground. The Zemindar wished to claim it for some feudal service, or under some pretence of landlord's dues. Perhaps the cunning Ryot—a very common occurrence—had taken advances and seed for the same piece of land from some other planter in the neighbourhood. What was to be done? There was law to be had. The planter might sue the Zemindar before the Zemindar's debtor, the judge, or he might sue the Ryot, and give occasion to some civilian to insult him, and to his police to victimize him. If he fell in with an independent and impartial judge he might even get a judgment in his favour. In the " Robert Watson and Co.'s Factories" there are, at this moment, 36,000 contracts for indigo, upon which advances have been made, the bulk of which vary from ten to twenty rupees. A pretty mass for the lengthy and technical operation of the old Company's courts, and a pretty harvest in the shape of stamp duties! Of course, recourse to law to recover advances, or enforce contracts, was never seriously thought of. But he had 20,000 of these contracts, and perhaps at least 5000 disputed cases. Even if he got a judgment it would be after fifteen months litigation, and in twenty-four hours the article in dispute would be perished. What did he do? He did what men at all times have done when the law afforded them no protec-

C

tion. He seized his right with a strong arm.* The planter and the Zemindar fought it out over the indigo patch. In those days there were men, called bludgeon men (lattials), maintained by the Zemindars to fight their quarrels. It was a profession which the planter found established, and again he fell into the habit of the country.

This is the plain truth concerning a scandal of other days, which existed about the same time as corruption existed in the Civil Service. A planter would now be ashamed to speak of *general* corruption in connection with the Civil Service, but Mr. Grant, with that exquisite taste for which he is so remarkable, does not fail to draw a sneer against the planters from those old lattial stories in his last Minute.

But if it were, even at the present day, as rife as it has been proved to be unknown—as rife as corruption and extortion at this moment confessedly are among the Government Police—whose fault would it be? Whose but that of the Government, which, by renouncing the first duties of government, that of protecting property, had remitted their Mofussil subjects to their natural rights?

Be it remembered, however, that with all these disputes the Ryot had nothing whatever to do. The fight

---

* The natives have two well known phrases for " doing oneself right by the strong arm" and "doing wrong by the strong arm." It is impossible to eradicate from the mind of the Bengali that the first is his indefeasible right, and we must always take this into consideration when we are judging of any rural conflict in India. All this is very graphically told by Mr. Seton Karr, in the article in the " Calcutta Review" for 1847, already cited; and wherein the young civilian's prejudices against the civil outlaw seem to contend against the young Englishman's sympathy with his own energetic and enterprising countryman. But Mr. Seton Karr had not then fallen into the jog-trot of office. In those days he had not learned to look for truth only through the refracting medium of the Civil Service.

was between Zemindars—native lords of manors—and Planters. The Ryot had his advances and his price, and grew his indigo : the contest was, who should have the plant when grown.

The Ryot had his grievances no doubt, as all people have their grievances under a bad Government. Just as the judge had and has, as he himself will be the first to confess and deplore—a corrupt set of officers (Omlah), who took bribes, and did with the ignorant judge as they listed ; just as the police exacted black mail from native cultivators and European settlers alike ; so the planter had his servants who cheated the Ryot, or cheated the planter, according to the capacity or willingness of the Ryot to make it worth their while to do so. But this is, and has been, the normal condition of India under the Company's system, and there is nothing exceptional in the matter.

It was under these discouragements that the factory we have been examining rose ; when the factor was the competitor of the Zemindar, the victim of the civilian, and a prey to the police. But time passed on, and, by the aid of the interference of the English nation, he was at last empowered to lease the rights of the Zemindar, to purchase and to hold land, to have legal rights, to buy the Zemindar out, to take leases of manors, to stand in the Zemindar's place. From that moment he became a more dangerous victim and a more difficult prey.

To understand this change, we must shortly recapitulate a few general facts.

The East India Company had the exclusive monopoly of the trade with India until 1814, notwithstanding many efforts to open the trade previous to that year.

The people of England were, in the ignorance which then prevailed, strangely persuaded by the Company, that if the trade to India were thrown open the price of goods in India would be so much enhanced by the competition of different traders, and their price in England would be so much diminished, that the freedom of the trade would end in the ruin of all who might adventure in it.

The rule of the Company was never very satisfactory to the British nation. Lord Cornwallis said, in 1789, that one-third of the Company's territory was a jungle for wild beasts. It was owing to this dissatisfaction that Mr. Fox brought forward his celebrated India Bill, which was lost. This failure was followed by the Bill of Mr. Pitt, which was carried, creating the Board of Control, but continuing the superintendence of all commercial matters, as formerly, in the hands of the Directors. The Company's Charter was prolonged until 1st March, 1814.

In Mr. Pitt's Act a kind of opening of the trade was made for private individuals, or "free merchants," who were allowed to export and import certain goods *in the Company's ships,* for carrying on which the Company were bound to provide 3000 tons annually, at a fixed scale per ton.

Few availed themselves of the privilege, exposed as they were to the ruinous competition of the Company, whose great object ever was—as we have already seen in their official correspondence—to keep the "interloper" out of India.

The Company's enemies did not increase to any extent. In 1807-8 the private imports into India, by private hands, were only £300,000.

The people of England at last moved with some

vigour, previous to the expiry of the Charter in 1814, to put an end to the trade monopoly; and they succeeded as regarded the trade with India, but the monopoly was continued as regarded the trade with China.

The chief conditions of the opening of the trade to India were that private individuals should confine themselves to the Presidencies of Calcutta, Madras, and Bombay, and Penang, in vessels of a certain tonnage, and that they were to be excluded from the ordinary trade, and the trade with China.

Thus emancipated, the private traders were not long in gaining the ascendancy: they, in a very few years, trebled the trade which the East India Company declared could not be extended, although, both in exports and imports, they were constantly subjected to heavy losses from the fitful competition and commercial speculations of the Company, who had Residents in all the principal towns, with a large staff of servants intended for coercive measures, when any interloper's interest clashed with the operations of the Company. Lord Wellesley then wrote "that the intimation of a wish from the Company's Resident is always received as a command by the native manufacturers and producers." And this holds true in India to this very day; and in such a case the unfortunate interloper must still go to the wall. It is now only on questions of official jealousy, or in the acquisition of land, that these parties can clash, for the Government is no longer a trader, and except in the unpopular, we may say hated, monopolies of opium and salt, it is no longer a manufacturer.

The capricious dealings of the old Company in commercial matters, after it had become exposed to competition, shewed heavy losses. When the Charter came to be renewed, in 1833, Parliament had therefore no hesitation in depriving the Company of its commercial character altogether, and in confining its government, for the future, to the territorial and political management of the country.

The new Charter extended to 1854, and, under it, any natural-born subject of England was entitled to proceed by sea to any port or place within the limit of the Company's Charter, having a custom-house establishment, and to reside thereat, or pass through any part of the Company's territories, to reside thereat.

Thus was the interloper gradually, and to a certain extent, emancipated.

We have already abundantly shewn that the Civil Service have as a body never ceased to throw every impediment in the way of settlers in the country. They latterly had not the same power of interference and annoyance to the interlopers who carried on commercial pursuits in the towns, but they had, and have, this power in the case of all Europeans who settle in the interior for the purpose of indigo planting. Indigo was the only agricultural produce in which European capital was embarked anterior to 1834, when the monopoly of the Company ceased, and when their silk filatures were sold, and their factories put up for sale.

In all these downward steps of the East India Company the British settler bore his part; ever crying aloud in England against the cruelty, rapacity, and oppression of the Company's rule; helping the agitators in England, and verifying the notion of Mr. Hawkins and the Civil Service generally, that the Planter was " an obstreperous gentleman."

The European settlers were not satisfied with a mere

theoretical victory. Day by day they became more active, more successful, and more hateful. They gained strength and independence as they increased at the Presidency towns and in the interior, and they necessarily became more obnoxious to the Civil Service, who found that the objects of their previous contempt had been the destroyers of their undivided supremacy. The " interlopers" were the first to move for the abolition of the Company in 1857, when the mutiny broke out. It was the interlopers who made so notorious in England the incompetency of the administration of the Company. The part taken by the indigo planters, and the other interlopers, in the agitation which resulted in the abolition of the Company, is still remembered. It certainly never will be forgiven by the old Directors of the defunct Company, or by the Civil Service, who, since then, have looked upon their exclusive privileges as doomed, and their dynasty as passing away. The bitter feud between them and the interloper is now, when public opinion runs against public castes, carefully disguised in words; and we gladly acknowledge that there are numerous instances of large minded men in that service who have overcome all their class prejudices and have opened their eyes to see the true interests of the country in which their lot has been thrown. But the old feud is burnt in upon the souls of fanatical civilians, such as Mr. Grant, and has become a yearning for a great revenge.

Such has been the progress of the owner of the house which we some pages back attempted to picture to the English reader. Thirty or forty years ago, when he first set foot in the country, he was nothing more than a Civil outlaw, seeking a spot whereon to fix an almost illicit manufacture. He bought a *potta* of 100 beegahs (33 acres), and built a factory, with vats, godowns, and machinery. But he could not buy it or hold it in his own name: he was an uncovenanted Englishman, and therefore *civiliter ex lex*. It was bought in the name of his native agent. The world was all against him: the Ryot was his only friend. How different is his position now! Allied with the Ryot, the European outlaw has been victorious. He has established his factory, he has bought out the Zemindar, he has become a rival in consequence and in influence to the Civil servant. By his own energy and perseverance, and by the support of the people of England, he has done this.

But the Indigo planter is become more than a planter. He is become a great landowner and a great reclaimer of the wastes. In 1829 there was a vehement contest between Lord William Bentinck and Sir C. Metcalfe, and the Directors of the Company, upon the question whether the planter should be allowed to hold land. We should much like to quote those state papers, but unhappily this, like all other Indian subjects, is too vast for the patience of the English public. The arguments used by the statesmen, and the querulous, and sometimes insolent replies of the Directors, are all extant in the volume to which we have already so often referred. It ended, however, in public opinion at home coming in to aid the Governor-General; and the planter was, in 1833, permitted to take the lands in his own name.

From that time forward the planter changed his character altogether. He was no longer only a planter: he was the lord of the manor, the landowner of the district. He either held direct from the Government, or rented of the native lord, the Zemindar, all his rents and feudal rights. In the latter case he paid the Zemindar much more than the current value, and he never enforced, or even asked for, those little feudal exactions upon marriages, births, deaths, and changes of occupancy, and other items, which amounted to a considerable sum in an aggregate of several thousand holdings.* He made his

---

* Again we cite the testimony of Mr. Seton Karr, when he had not to draw a damnatory Indigo Report. He then wrote, when indigo abuses were only just dying out:—

"Nowhere has the contrast between European energy and Asiatic torpor been so signally displayed. Year after year the Zemindar, following obsequiously in the path of his ancestors, had seen the same patch of jungle growing up, which at best could only furnish materials for mats, or a cottage thatch. In some cases he had looked on where Nature had even advanced and cultivation receded from her empire; but when the native gazed in apathy, the new settler began to clear away. We could mention numerous instances where the rule of the planter has been attended with the extension of agriculture, and consequent benefit to the Ryot; but one example will suffice, as it illustrates most clearly the difference between the Oriental and British character. A ravine, or rather the bend of a river, had in process of time been filled up by a yearly alluvial deposit, and as new and fertile land was immediately claimed by two old belligerents. After the usual amount of disputes the quarrel was terminated by the authorities: a boundary line was drawn exactly down the middle of the old bed of the river, and an equal half thus secured to both. But now came the difference in the use made of the acquisition. The Zemindar had been as anxious in the pursuit of his object as the most ardent European: he had contested every point, and given up nothing, even to the last. But he had no intention of deriving benefit himself, or allowing others to derive any from what it had cost him so much to gain. Months and months the land lay fallow, and the increasing jungle sprung up. But the planter, in the course of two years, had nearly the whole in cultivation, and when we last visited the place it was already sprouting with the promise of an excellent crop. It seemed as if the boundary-line drawn by the Deputy-Collector had realized the old story of the knife, which on one side was impregnated with poison and withered all it touched, on the other bestowed healing juices and the vigorous sap of life."— *Calcutta Review,* vol. vii. p. 27.

"The leaseholder, or the '*putnidar,*' forbears to put in force the power derived by him to measure and assess the lands of the Ryots to the full amount legally permissible; and he also never calls on the Ryots for those various payments which some of the native Zemindars, on some one pretext or other, constantly demand from the tenants on births, marriages, religious festivals, and similar events, or on pressing necessities. Mr. J. P. Wise asserted his belief that he could double the rent

profit, however, by clearing the jungle, and bringing whole plains of wilderness into cultivation. A certain portion, perhaps one-twentieth of the whole, he kept for indigo cultivation, or let upon that condition; the rest he let to the natives upon moderate rents. In all probability the factory town which we have described was, twenty-five years ago, upon the edge of a wild-beast covert. It is a matter of universal notoriety among the dwellers in the present district of Nuddea or Kishnaghur, that, twenty-five years ago, one-third of that great indigo district was jungle. The chief factory-house in another district is even now called by a name which indicates the abundance of wild beasts in the neighbourhood, being formed from the Bengali word " to hunt."*

The planter is now just in the position of a lessee of church lands in England, except that the Zemindar is very generally engaged in intriguing among the Ryots, and using his hereditary influence among them to thwart his European lessor, generally with one object—to extort a bribe. He is often successful, for he knows very well that indigo is the planter's weak point, and that there are a hundred days in every year when the planter is at every one's mercy; when Lieutenant-Governor, Zemindar, Civil servant, and policeman, must all be propitiated in their own different ways; and when a cessation of labour for twenty-four hours is ruin.

We have already quoted the opinion of Lord William Bentinck, after inquiry made, as to the manner in which

of his Ryots; and Mr. Forlong said that he allowed the Ryots to sit at as easy a rate as possible. Mr. Larmour, in Mulnath alone, has released 17,000 beegahs of land, held rent free, on the production by the holder of certain papers, called the toidad, endorsed by the collector of revenue."—*Report of the Indigo Committee,* 1860, par 17.

* This factory is in Rajshahye, and called " Shikarpore."

the planter, even in his day, used the influence his position gave him.   We have also quoted the unwilling testimony of Mr. Walters, the magistrate of Dacca, to the
fact that the planters are held in much estimation by the
natives, are called upon to arbitrate disputes, are dispensers of medicine to the sick, are advisers of those in difficulty, advance money to those in need on the occasion of
family events which would otherwise involve them for life
with native money-lenders, and are constantly attending
to the wants and wishes of their poor neighbours.   The
same facts are grudgingly admitted even by this Indigo
Commission.   In fact, every inquiry made, by either friend
or enemy, has eventuated in the same admission, that the
planter in his district performs the same offices in his
neighbourhood that an English landed proprietor does
upon his estate.   "No thanks to him," say men like Mr.
J. P. Grant.   "It is to his interest to do so : if he did
not, he would not get his indigo."   This is true : the law
gives him no protection.   What would an English landlord or contractor think if he was told that the law was
open to him for breaches of contract, and found that this
"law" consisted of a right to file 36,000 Bills in Chancery
against 36,000 cottagers who had been incited by the
executive authorities of the country to violate their contracts and to strike work?   It is true, as the white Brahmin caste insists, that benevolence is the planter's interest.
But how complete an answer is this to all other general
charges?   and what can savour more of the age of gold in
these degenerate days than that a trade should flourish
upon moral influence alone, and that it should be made a
charge against the trader that he works up this moral
influence by means of acts of benevolence?

   We should like to see Mr. J. P. Grant left to " moral

influence" to manufacture his opium, or to work his salt monopoly. We would look indulgently upon his doing so by any acts of benevolence which his policy might dictate.

And yet Mr. Grant, as a man of the world, wonders that while the majority of the planter class act thus, there sometimes occurs the exception of a foolish planter, who, in the absence of law, will right himself by force, rather than by what was, before Mr. Grant came upon the scene, the far more effectual and more common means of acts of good neighbourship !

Before we proceed to notice the business arrangements between the planters and the Ryots, it will be well to say a few words upon the value and quantity of the indigo produced in India.

CHAPTER IV.

THE INDIGO PRODUCE OF INDIA.

LET us now contemplate for a moment the quantity and value of the produce which factories like those we have been examining turn out annually.

Indigo planting in Bengal is an old child of the Company. Before the renewal of the Charter, in 1834, the private adventurer, in his eagerness to take shelter in the shadow of some potent civilian, associated himself with some fortunate mortal who was covenanted to the Company. The civilian lent money to the planter, either at interest or on condition of his having a certain share in the profits. At one time civilians openly carried on factories in their own names. Being the official of the district they carried every thing their own way with the Ryots.

This explains why the production of indigo in Bengal has so greatly varied from time to time. The capricious operations of the Company when they came into the Calcutta market as buyers in competition with private traders ran up prices so high on several occasions, that the planters were induced to extend their cultivation, forgetting that the article was one of limited demand or consumption, and that, when the supply exceeded what is called the effectual demand, lower prices must be the consequence, according to the laws of trade.

The production of indigo in Bengal (including Tirhoot and the North-West indigo districts), in 1819, 1820, and

1822, was on an average about 70,000 maunds (of 72 lbs.), and in 1826 the production rose to 144,000 maunds, which was the largest crop during the period of the existence of the Company's commercial monopoly.   In the following year, 1827, the crop in Bengal was only 90,000 maunds.   The largest crops of indigo ever known were in 1843 and 1844, when Bengal produced 165,000, and 172,050 maunds.   In 1846 the crop was 90,000 maunds, and for the last five years the average crop may be taken at 105,000 maunds.

Madras, which in former years produced little or no indigo, has been exporting largely of the dye of late years, its annual exports being now, on an average of the last five years, say 28,000 maunds.

Taking the average exports
    From Bengal at .   .   .   105,000 maunds.
    And from Madras   .   .   28,000   „
    _____
    The total exports were   .   133,000   „

They send a few maunds of coarse indigo from Bombay not worth taking into calculation.

So much for quantity.   Now for value.

The prices of indigo have been very fluctuating in the markets of India and Europe.   Not many years ago fine Bengal indigo sold as low as 140 and 150 rupees per maund, the same quality of indigo which has been selling in Calcutta, for the last two or three years, at 220 to 240 rupees per maund ; and this year fine Bengal indigo may realize about the former figure.   There are many circumstances to affect prices up or down ; the quantity produced yearly; the consumption and stock in the markets to which the article is exported ; and the condition of trade and the money market, as well as the aspect from time to time of European politics.

The price in England in 1826 was 12s, and in 1827 13s per pound for fine Bengal indigo.

In 1846 it fell to 5s 6d, and in 1848 and 1849 was 5s 9d per pound.

Since 1852 prices have gradually risen. In 1858 fine indigo fetched as high as 9s 6d per pound. But the same quality may now be had at 7s 6d to 8s per pound.

The value of the block of the indigo concerns in Bengal, or the price at which they stand in the books of the planters or proprietors, is estimated, as we have already seen, at seven or eight millions sterling.

The annual outlay for the cultivation of indigo in Bengal varies from one-and-half to two millions, *all of which is circulated in the indigo districts.*

In the Indigo Commission Report it is stated that the value of the block belonging to Messrs. I. and R. Watson and the Bengal Indigo Company is £500,000, or half-a-million sterling.

In further proof of the value of this manufacture to the district where it exists, we find it stated, in the same Report, that *in one district* the money annually expended on indigo cultivation is £60,000, in excess of the total land rent which the same district yields annually to Government : and this, let it be remembered, is only one of the articles produced from the soil, from an area, as the Report states, not exceeding *one-sixteenth to one-twentieth* of the average cultivation of every Ryot in the district; the rest of his land, to the extent of fifteen-sixteenths or nineteen-twentieths, being under other crops, and he has the use of the indigo lands, unless he keeps them for indigo-seed, after the plant is cut in June and July.

CHAPTER V.

THE PLANTER AND THE RYOTS.

WITHIN two years of the present date, nothing in India was so comfortable as the relations between an indigo-planter and his Ryots. In India, where nothing is true and every thing is in dispute, it is wonderful how this fact stands out conspicuous in the midst of every inquiry, and emerges from every report. We do not mean to say that this course of true love was without any ripple. Just as every native, and even every Civil servant, has for many years been complaining that the Company's judge is surrounded by an "omlah," or set of subordinate officers, who cheat and extort and environ the most well-intentioned civilian with an impenetrable fortification of corrupt underlings—making the judicature of India one atmosphere of perjury and bribery—so the planter is obliged to have his "omlah," who make the most of their opportunities. Just as the "omlah" of the Government collectors in the Presidency of Madras have been proved to have committed acts of torture, so the native collectors of the planter may sometimes have been guilty, not of any such acts as these—God forbid!—but of acts of fraud and violence to obtain what was their master's right. The planter cannot pretend to be free from a vice of Indian society from which the Governor-General himself can claim no immunity. The native servants of the factory *will* take bribes. They will for a bribe measure out land for indigo which is useless for that or for any other purpose, and they will, in revenge for not receiving a bribe, measure out the land most disadvantageous to the Ryot to part with, and most disadvantageous to the planter to receive. They will for a bribe put the measuring-cord round the expanded heads of the Indigo bundles, or, in revenge for not receiving a bribe, round the waists of the bundles. They will, when it is possible, note down some of the bundles of the man who has not bribed them to the score of another man who has. They will favour all sorts of tricks against their employer, or they will invent frauds which do not exist. The planter is an energetic, active man, aware of all these dangers, and always on the watch for them, and he has usually an European assistant as watchful as himself: yet they will occur,—not constantly and habitually as they do in the Court of the trusting and uninformed civilian, but they will sometimes occur.

Allowing, however, as men of common sense will always allow, for the surrounding circumstances, the relation between the planter and the Ryots was the most satisfactory of any relation between Europeans and natives in India.

After the close of the manufacturing season the planter's object is to make sure of his indigo. He is surrounded by swarms of little farmers with their small "jummas"—a sort of copyholds or customary freeholds—of from five to fifty acres, who have come to settle accounts and to take fresh advances for the ensuing season. Thousands are ready to take the money. Perhaps, as the report of Mr. Grant's secretary, sitting as president of the Indigo Commissioners, 1860, admits, "it is a season of the year when the Ryot is in want of money for rent and for the annual festival of Doorga. Advances are in some instances willingly and even greedily accepted.

D

Some men are in debt; others want to spend money, and all like money without interest."* Some, also, are doubtless in debt to the factory. It is a debt they never intend to pay; but it will happen in India, as in other places, that a debt occasions a certain state of obligation, and, as the planter is well aware that it is useless to ask for his debt, and equally useless to expect his indigo without advancing the usual money and seed, the debtor agrees for a certain quantity of indigo, and goes and enjoys himself at his Doorga feast; † acting pretty much, as Macaulay says the second Pitt acted when, being in debt to his coachmaker, he ordered another carriage.

How much better it would be if there were no feast of Doorga, and if the Ryots wanted no advances, and if the Ryots would grow the indigo, and then at the proper time offer it to the competing planters. So say certain intensely wise men, simpletons of the first order, who are half inclined to think with Alfonso the Wise—that conceited blasphemer, who remarked that it was rather a pity he had not been present at the creation; for that he might have given a hint or two which would have prevented many incongruities. Mr. Grant is also quite of opinion that the Ryot and the planter are very wrong, and that the Ryot ought to grow and sell, and get the full market price for his produce.‡ Among the barren

---

* Report, par. 57.

† " On all domestic occurrences, births, deaths and marriages, a native is put to a great expense, and cannot get on without the aid of a banker —and this from the Rajah to the lowest peasant. And they prefer dealing with the indigo manufacturer, who charges no interest, to any other person."

‡ " If the planter had paid, in cash, such a price for indigo-plant as would have made it more profitable to the Ryot to grow that crop than any other, abstaining also from all molestation of the Ryot by himself, or his servants, no one pretends that the planter would not have got, year after year, as much indigo-plant as he could pay for."—*Mr. Grant's Minute upon the Indigo Planter's petition against him.*

platitudes with which Mr. Grant's Minute abounds, this
is conspicuous. It is like a suggestion that the moon
should be lit up all the month through. It is the most
inane of truisms. Of course we all think this. Nothing
would delight us more than a full supply of indigo-plant
ready when we want it, at the market-price. Undoubtedly it would be much better if the Ryots would grow
their indigo and never run in debt, and if Mr. Pitt had
paid his coachbuilder's bill, and had not ordered a carriage he did not want. But unfortunately both the Indian farmer and the British minister had habits of personal expenditure which had not the character of fore-
thought. Mr. Pitt had no money to pay his coachmaker,
and Bonomallee Mundle has no money to pay his rent
and provide indigo-seed. Instead of getting as much
indigo-plant as he could pay for, the planter would not
by any such means, get a single bundle. He might
as well go into a bazaar at Kishnaghur for a choice of
golden statues. No one knows this better than Mr.
Grant. He knows that the men whom he insists upon
calling "*capitalists*" have not a copper pice to call their
own. He knows, also, that in India nothing is ever done
without "advances;" that if he wants a Government
work done, he must pay by advances; that if he wants
a cart mended, he must pay by advances; and that when
he wants poppies grown for opium, he invariably pays
by advances. In attempting to poison the ministerial
mind at home against the Indigo system, he knows very
well that he is calumniating a system which he himself
is using in an aggravated form every day of his life. In
talking about "paying in cash such a price for indigo-
plant," he is using a disingenuous artifice, and taking ad-

vantage of the presumed ignorance in England of Indian habits.

The contracts are made, and the advances are paid over.

The advance varies from two to three rupees a beegah. The crop ought to be, if the land be good and the culture careful, from fifteen to twenty-five (say twenty as an average) bundles per beegah.

The payment at present varies from a rupee for four bundles to a rupee for six bundles.

The advance covers nearly all the expected profit of the Ryot except the cold-weather crop of linseed or mustard, which he grows for himself after the indigo is cut.

The weeding, when the land is kept clear, as it is in Kishnaghur or Jessore, is nearly nominal; and the seed obtainable from the second cuttings far more than compensates for the labour of weeding.

Indigo is a crop of the easiest possible cultivation, so far as mere labour is concerned; but it requires the greatest tenderness of supervision, and the occasional glance of the European eye.

When the Ryot has spent his advance in paying the Zemindar his rent, or in celebrating his Poojah, it is very likely that he will have no money-balance to receive out of his indigo crop. It is possible, that if he has cultivated his land badly, or sold half his seed, or baked his seed before sowing it, in order to sow a crop of his own upon the land, and throw the blame on the planter's seed—it is possible in many of these cases that the balance may be against him; but as there is no instance of any Ryot ever paying up, or ever being sued for any such balance, this will not much affect his happiness, except so far as it may

affect his receipts in a good year.* The worst of the
matter is, as Mr. Grant has so sagaciously discovered,
that he cannot go to market with the indigo, for that he
has already sold it and spent the money.

In fact, the Ryot cannot in ordinary seasons, " eat his
cake and have it too." This is what, either as a pretence

---

* Mr. Larmour, the manager of some of the most extensive and
valuable indigo properties in Bengal, in his evidence before " the Indigo
Committee, 1860," describes the result to the Ryots in a good year:—
" *Mr. Sale.*] Q. Are we to understand that the Ryot is in debt to the
factory, and to the native banker who makes advances on the rice crop,
and frequently under the supervision of both parties at the same time?
" A. Many Ryots are indebted both to the manhajun and the factory.
" Q. Is it not frequently the case that the Ryot is bound to deliver
his surplus crop to the mahajun at fixed price under the market rate?
" It is the custom for the Ryot to deliver all his rice crop to the mahajun, who generally fixes his own price upon it, deducting fifty per cent.
for the advance made. That is, if he has advanced one maund to the
Ryot, he receives in return for that one, one maund and a half.
" *The Baboo.*] Q. You have stated that, after passing of Act XI.
[the Temporary Summary Remedies Act, passed for six months, and
now expired], Ryots, who never held advances before, came forward and
received their advances willingly ; can you state what number of Ryots
have thus willingly taken advances, and to cultivate what quantity of
lands ?
" A. About eight or ten Ryots—I don't exactly recollect the number
—offered to cultivate ten beegahs of land at an advance of two rupees
per beegah.
" Q. Is the cultivation of indigo profitable or otherwise to the Ryots ?
" A. That depends entirely upon the season. In the last season, at
the Mulnauth factory the average return per beegah was 14 bundles
per beegah. Upwards of 100 Ryots cut more than 20 bundles per
beegah ; 237 Ryots cleared off their advances and debt to the factory,
and received *fazil*, or excess payments. The return of 20 bundles
per beegah pays a Ryot well, apart from the indigo-seed which he also
gets from the stumps. [Mr. Larmour here filed a paper in English,
referring to the books in original, which he also filed.]
" *The Baboo.*] Q. What number of indigo Ryots is there in the Mulnauth factory ?
" A. One thousand three hundred and seventy-eight.
" Q. You have stated that out of 1378 Ryots, 237 had cleared their
advances ; could you state how the accounts of the remaining Ryots
stand ?
" A. For the last eight years in Kishnaghur the indigo cultivation has

for an ulterior purpose, or as an honest craze, people like
Mr. Grant, and Mr. Potter of the London Trades'
Unions, are always crying for.   It is for want of in-
struction probably ; but it is very expensive to keep
Indian Governors and London working-men so ignorant.

The indigo part of the Ryot's farm is the part which
yields him his little ready money.   He gets this without
interest.   Don't, however, let it be supposed that the rice
is grown out of the Ryot's own " capital."   He gets
advances also upon his rice before he puts a plough into
the ground ; but he gets these from the native money-
lender at from 50 to 100 per cent., and he knows very
well that if he does not keep time with this unrelenting
creditor, he will be sold up without mercy.   As to the
planter, all that he has to fear is a certain sort of unde-
fined obligation to sow some indigo for him next year,
whether he may like it or not.   It is not wonderful, therefore, that the Ryot should slip into arrears with his
easiest creditor, and that the books of every factory should
shew thousands of columns of arrears, which Mr. Grant
taunts the planters with being, together with their vats,
their only capital.

been very disastrous.   The remainder of the Ryots did not clear off the
balances and debt in full, and consquently had no excess to receive.

"Q. Have these 237 Ryots entered into fresh engagements this year ?

"A. Every Ryot in the Mulnauth concern, amounting to 11,000,
entered into new engagements, and fulfilled them.

" *Mr. Fergusson*] Q. Have you had occasion to sue any single Ryot
in the Mulnauth concern for breach of contract? ,

"A. In no single instance.

" Q. Have the Ryots in the Baraset concern renewed their engagements, and sown indigo as usual, or had you to sue them there?

"A. The Ryots in the Baraset concern have this year engaged and
sown their indigo to the extent of 5000 beegahs, half the former cultivation of the concern.   Last year the concern was closed.   I have had no
occasion to carry out any case against the Ryots of that concern under
the new Act."

Let us hasten to say — for presently Mr. Grant will very likely affirm that we are seeking power to sell up every one of these Ryots—that we are not asking for any summary remedy as to these arrears. The worst thing an indigo planter could do for his own interest would be to ruin a Ryot. All we are asking is, for lawful protection against fraud, as when a Ryot takes advances from more than one planter, or takes the planter's money and seed, and does not sow the land.

Let us admit, also, that if a Ryot were, as Mr. Grant, with that tremendous assurance of his, avers him to be, a capitalist, he very possibly might not just now sow indigo. There are a great many things which a man does, and which he would not do if he could live without doing them.   Mr. Grant's punkawallah would not pull his punkah all the hot night through, if impecuniosity did not compel him to do it.   These things are not confined to India. The same necessity is felt in England. John Barleycorn the publican has just got into possession of a very handsome public-house. It required more capital than John Barleycorn had at his banker's, and the owners of the new house were Messrs. Double-ex the brewers. So John Barleycorn took " advances" from Messrs. Double-ex, and gives them a bond for repayment. Now when John Barleycorn begins to sell his beer he finds that he could drive a more profitable trade if he could have his beer from Messrs. Treble-ex rather than from Messrs. Double-ex. But then there is his bond and his " arrears." He knows very well that if one of the Messrs. Treble-ex's drays were seen at his door, the Double-exes would call in their advances, and, when his bond was produced in an English court of law, Lord Palmerston or Sir G. Lewis would not come down to Westminster Hall and tell the judges how hard it is that the Double-exes should insist upon Barleycorn dealing with those who had advanced him wherewith to go into business; nor would the chief commissioner of police volunteer his advice to publicans to buy their beer just where they pleased. The recalcitrant Barleycorn would infallibly be sold up, and every one would say it served him right for his bad faith and his ingratitude.

So with the bakers and the millers, and so with the merchants and the bill-discounters, and so with every class of debtors and creditors all over the world; but especially and above all, so with Mr. Grant's poppy-growing Ryots, who could sell their opium for just 600 per cent. more to other people than the price at which Mr. Grant compels them to sell it to him.

But why does the Ryot rather reluctantly engage himself to sow one-twentieth part of his land with indigo? For very varied reasons. There is a prejudice against the Double-ex beer, and there is a prejudice against indigo. It was said of Coleridge, that whenever an act assumed the form of a duty, it became impossible for him to perform it: so of a Hindoo or a Mussulman it may be said, that whenever an act assumes the form of an obligation, he hates it; but if it assume the form of an obligation, the price of which has already been received, he abhors it. In trying to break his agreements he has got into many scrapes, and has fallen into many arrears; but having still been unable to learn that honesty is the best policy, he hates an obligation which he knows he shall be tempted—having spent the advance—to avoid, and which he knows also he will be held to, in default of law, by some means or other to perform. He would like to have all the benefits of the neighbouring factory, and avoid any return. He would like the medicine, the free loans, the protection, the help when his rice crops fail, and the advances; but when he has secured all this, he would rather not grow the indigo;* especially if some Missionary or magistrate, still more if the Sircar [Go-

* These circumstances are stated in the Report on "The Conduct of Europeans in India," (p. 161), compiled from returns from the Civil servants in the Mofussil, supplied in answer to Lord William Bentinck's circular. The Report was made for the use of the Board of Control.

"The Ryot receives advances for the cultivation of indigo, and either neglects to plough his land, or, when he has ploughed it, refuses to sow it at the proper season with indigo: and perhaps sows instead, rice, barley, sugar, or some other crop, for his own use.

"Sometimes the seed received from the planter is parched before it is sown, to destroy its germinative power, and after sufficient time has been allowed to elapse for the growth of good seed, the land is resown by the Ryot with some other crop, and the failure of the indigo is attributed to the badness of the seed furnished by the planter. At other times the indigo seed is ploughed up by the Ryot, or the seed of other crops sown with or upon it.

"Advances are received in respect of land to which the Ryot has no title, or of which he is but a joint tenant. Land to which the title is doubtful is frequently offered to the planter with a view of interesting him in supporting the claim of the party from whom he obtained the land. And advances are constantly received from two planters for the same crop: in which case, when the indigo is fit to be cut a dispute arises between them respecting their respective rights to the crop.

"The Zemindars, and sometimes the native officers of the court, with a view to extract bribes from the planter, employ their influence with the Ryots, to induce them to combine and refuse to cultivate the land for which they have received advances. For this purpose, *bonds not to cultivate indigo are frequently taken by the Zemindar from the Ryots.* In other cases they erect factories, and compel the Ryots to receive advances from them, though already under agreement to cultivate the same land for other planters. Here, as before, the object in view frequently is to obtain money from the planters, and not to manufacture indigo.

"Sometimes they lease villages to the factories, and refuse, after they have received the advance agreed upon, to deliver them up. In other cases, though they deliver them up the villages, they instigate the Ryots to stop the planter's ploughs when he proceeds to till the land, and sometimes they collect large bodies of men together, to prevent the planter from cultivating even that land which he has obtained from other parties.

"In one case a Zemindar and a planter seem to have raised a com-

vernment] itself, should suggest to him that he need not complete his contract unless he likes, and should remind him that there is no law to make him.

The land applicable to indigo is that which is least valuable for rice cultivation. More than one-half of the indigo crop in Lower Bengal is sown upon new alluvial formed lands, or churs, on the banks of the large rivers or beds of old rivers which are unfit for rice or any other crop. Moreover, indigo is a fertilizing and not an exhausting crop. What is the best land for rice? The Ryot will tell you "The rich strong black loam." Nine-

---

bination of 7000 men, who agreed not to sow indigo themselves, and to prevent other Ryots from sowing it, for a certain British factory.

"When the season arrives for ploughing the land, the Ryots who have agreed to cultivate indigo for the factory neglect to plough, or the planter finds a body of men assembled to prevent him from ploughing that of which he has obtained leave for home cultivation. Sometimes the land, instead of being retained for indigo, is sown with rice or other crops for the Ryot's own use; still more frequently the land is properly prepared by the Ryots, but when the rains commence and the seed should be sown, some or all of the Ryots refuse or neglect to sow. ' The sowing of indigo admits of no delay: when the land is prepared for the reception of the seed, no time must be lost. Delay, that in all cases is dangerous, in this is ruinous: either the lands must be sown at once, or not at all.' The planter has made advances, not only to the owners or occupiers of the land, but frequently to the labourers whom he had expected to employ during the season of manufacture. His factory, with its establishment, have been kept up at great expense; *the law does not even profess to afford him assistance,* except to recover his advances, and even these he can never hope to obtain, in consequence of the poverty of the Ryots. *During the delay necessary to procure the assistance of the Court, the season would pass away, and leave the planter perhaps wholly ruined.*   *   *   *   *   *

"Of Allyghur, the Commissioner of the Moradabad division says, 'So far as my experience goes, and it is founded on a residence of six years, in a district (Allyghur) filled with indigo planters, I have found the lower classes of the natives better clothed, richer, and more industrious in the neighbourhood of the factories than those at a distance; and at the same time I cannot bring to my recollection a single instance of a native having suffered cruelty or oppression from an indigo planter or his servants.' "

tenths of this is bheel land, which is land on which indigo is never sown. The planter aims at having a proportion of various descriptions of soil, so that, whatever
may be the weather, he may make an average, and have
a chance of a good crop. It is not, therefore, from any
fear of losing his best rice land that the Ryot can object
to sow indigo.

Indigo is, no doubt, like opium, a precarious crop ;
and one or two bad seasons may disgust a whole country
side. But the same accidents happen to rice * Do we
not in England hear every now and then of failures of
the rice crops, and wide-spread famine in Bengal? How
often is the rice entirely ruined by inundation? and how
often has it happened that the "aous" rice, or that
grown on high land—the only land on which indigo and
rice will both grow—is a failure? We have known Ryots
for several consecutive years, realize less than a rupee
and a-half from their aous paddy. In those years of
famine the little indigo patch is the plant which saves
the poor Ryot, and the factory is his only friend †

This fact is forcibly confessed in that article in the
Calcutta Review for January, 1847, from which we have
before quoted.

" We will contrast," says the writer, " the condition of

---

* The Ryots frequently lose their rice crop from long drought, too
much rain, or an early and sudden inundation ; when they are obliged
to sell their cattle, or ask assistance from the planters.

† Whenever a Jumma or small holding of land becomes vacant in any
of the villages, there are numerous petitions from new Ryots for the
lands,—who invariably agree to sow a certain extent of land with indigo
—upon condition of getting that Jumma.

Also, when a property is bought by a planter with the power of
measuring and re-assessing the lands,—in arranging a moderate assessment with the Ryots, they agree to sow a certain extent of the lands
with indigo,—as the planter relinquishes his fair profit from the property,
for the consideration of the indigo cultivation.

" a Ryot who sows both indigo and rice with that of one
" who confines himself solely to the latter. When the
" rains fall too rapidly, and the rice crop is literally
" drowned, nothing can be more pitiable than the state of
" the cultivator of rice alone. His daily bread is gone,
" and he must sell his bullocks, and steal, starve, or earn
" a precarious subsistence by taking service, or by handi-
" craft. He is deeply in debt to the mahajun, or money-
" lender, and this worthy invariably commences to exact
" his dues, by laying hold of his oxen and his cows. But
" suppose the Ryot, out of eight beegahs to have given
" up two to indigo. His rice crop is gone, and the indigo
" produce is only middling, but still the very dependence
" on the factory is a relief. The very thing which in a
" good season, and in his old independent state, was his
" great curse, in the evil day becomes almost a blessing.
" He may borrow, too, from the planter, and the latter
" will lend from feelings in which interest certainly has a
" large share, but from which benevolence and honesty of
" purpose is not wholly excluded. Although it may be
" argued that to lend to the Ryots only secures the
" planter's hold over him, that in a few rupees given in
" the time of want is an earnest of his sowing two or
" more additional beegahs in March or April; yet we
" would willingly believe that there are men whose con-
" duct in such instances is regulated by the compassion,
" the sincerity, and the kindness of Christians."

What consequence what the man's motives may be?—
he saves these people from starving. Of course a planter,
as well as a Lieutenant-Governor, or a Lieutenant-Governor's secretary, has his natural feelings when his fel-
low-creatures are dying about him; but *we* venture to
hope that, in addition to " the compassion, the sincerity,

and the kindness of a Christian," he finds his own mercantile return in what he does. If he does, he can repeat the acts, and can do them upon a large scale; if he does not, no motives can enable him to bear up long against the loss, or to repeat that loss as the occasions recur. This is a hypocritical whine borrowed from the planters' bitter foes. When, to avoid public execration, they who never move a finger to help the native in his dire distresses, and to whom in their chairs of office the salt Ryot in his agony looks in vain for "the compassion, the sincerity, and the kindness of the Christian," are obliged to admire the planters' acts : they indemnify themselves by depreciating his motives. But, granting the worst that can be said, what must be the value to the rural districts of India of a class of men whose "interested" motives are admitted by their enemies to produce these results ?

All crops are uncertain in a tropical country, where vegetation depends on rains and rivers: but it is not because indigo sometimes fails that the Ryot prefers rice.

Nor is it because rice has been more remunerative. Let us examine this matter. We are speaking now, be it remembered, of the state of things two years ago.

Indigo is sown with little trouble, and weeded for less : when ripe, it is cut and brought to the factory, sometimes by the Ryot, and sometimes by the factory. The same piece of land will require double the attention if cultivated for paddy. In the rice cultivation weeding is laborious and expensive ; nor is the expense over with the reaping : the paddy must be threshed, and in many cases, when ready for market, it has to be made over to the mahajun at the rate of one and a-half to one and three-quarter maunds for every maund advanced a few months previously. It must be remembered, also, that fresh good rice is returned, probably, for musty stuff that has been rotting in the *golah*. There are few planters who have not had paddy, literally black, brought to them by the Ryots, and their interference sought to secure the boon of being allowed to return only one and a quarter maund of good, for each maund of bad paddy received four months before, the price of good grain at both periods being about the same. Take a piece of land with the cold weather crop just off it, and the expenses for growing both paddy and indigo fairly set down, are about as follows : —

Expenses of Aous Paddy.				*Expenses of Indigo.*			
Ploughing .	.	.	Rs. 1 8	Ploughing.	.	.	Rs. 1 0
Harrowing .	.	.	,, 0 2	Weeding .	.	.	,, 0 6
Beeda ditto.	.	.	,, 0 2	Cutting‡ .	.	.	,, 0 6
Weeding .	.	.	,, 1 4	Carriage§ .	.	.	,, 0 6
Cutting* .	.	.	,, 0 12	Seed .	.	.	,, 0 4
Threshing, &c.	.	.	,, 0 4	Rent‖ .	.	.	,, 1 0
Seed† .	.	.	,, 0 12				
Rent .	.	.	,, 1 0			Total ,,	3 0
	Total	,,	5 12				

Let us suppose a full crop of both, say six rupees worth of paddy, and reckoning twenty bundles of indigo at four per rupee, five rupees for the indigo : the former thus leaves a balance of four annas ; the latter, of two rupees. The account will stand thus : --

* We reckon the money value of the sheaves allowed to the reapers.

† Seed for rice—15 seers per biggah is sown ; but the Ryot pays for *double* to the Mahajun.

‡ In Watson's and some other concerns "cutting" is paid by the factory.

§ In some factories—indeed, in most—the carriage is paid by the planter.

‖ Rents.—On the banks of the Ganges, the rent of a beegah of land is only 6 to 8 annas for *two crops ;* for indigo, 4 *annas.*

Aous Paddy.				*Indigo.*			
Value of crop	.	. Rs.	6 0	Value of crop	.	. Rs.	5 0
Cost of production	.	,,	5 12	Cost of production	.	,,	3 0
	Profit	,,	0 4		Profit	,,	2 0

We refer here to " aous " paddy, viz. that sown on high land suitable to indigo. The " ammon " is far more profitable, and is sown in *bheels*, &c., where indigo cannot grow.

The contract* which is signed, or otherwise authenticated on the advance being made, is of the simplest kind. It is either for two or five years. It provides penalties in case of non-fulfilment, and in most cases sets out the boundaries of the land on which the indigo shall be grown. The contract is entered in the factory books, and below the entry is jotted the Ryot's account for every year— cash paid and plant delivered ; the seed being charged at an unvarying sum, which is seldom more than one-

* *Mr. President.*] Q. For what period of years is your contract?

A. The contracts are generally for three years, but are renewed every year on a fresh stamp.

Mr. Temple.] Q. Are these contracts duly filled in at the time the engagements are entered into ?

A. No. The contracts are not filled up on the day the engagement is made, in the instance of every Ryot. The advances of a factory are generally made in two or three days : it would be an impossibility to write up these contracts within that time, and it is only with the engagement of the head Ryots that the contracts are filled up.

Q. But then do the contracts of the subordinate or smaller Ryots remain unwritten ?

A. Yes, they generally do ; very few are able to write, and it is considered a mere matter of form. *No person has ever dreamt of taking a Ryot into court to recover his balance.*

Q. Do the stamp papers for these contracts remain in the factory ?

A. It has been an infatuation that the planters laboured under, that redress could be had against a Ryot in a civil court, and they have kept up appearances by renewing their engagements with the Ryots on stamp paper.—*Mr. Larmour's Evidence before the Indigo Commissioners,* 1860.

fourth of the current price.   It is true that the account
is often embarrassed with the amount of loans advanced
in times of dire necessity, to pay the pressing Zemindar's
rent, or to purchase bullocks to work their rice lands, or
to recover their bullocks when they have been seized.
These are the large items which bring the Ryot into
debt with the factory; and the planter has lent the
money, not entirely out of Christian kindness it must be
admitted, but to prevent the man being ruined by recourse to the native money-lender, and thus rendered
unable to perform his indigo contracts.   Imagine then
the consequence of removing out of the rural districts of
Bengal (where capital is so scarce, and even a rupee is
so large a sum), an annual two millions of money thus
employed!   Yet this is what Mr. Grant is now calmly
contemplating as the result of his agitation!   What shall
we say of the intellect or of the honesty of purpose of a
man who can premeditate such an act as this, and ask
the English Government to believe that his object is the
advantage of the natives!

   We must follow out the relations of the planter and
Ryot to the vat; and this harvest home has been so very
well described in an article in the *Calcutta Review* for
March 1858, that we cannot do so well as to borrow the
writer's language, even at the expense of reiterating some
things we have before said.   When the indigo is ripe for
cutting, it is cut and carried, sometimes by the Ryot,
generally by the planter's servants.   In the former case
" the Ryot brings his plant to the factory; the mohurrir,
" or rather the mohurrirs, for it is the general custom to
" have two, write down the number of sheaves as counted
" before the Ryot—the number which go to the bundle,
" and the number of bundles.   If the Ryot is not satis-

" fied with the mohurrir's estimate, the sheaves are mea-
" sured with the chain. The name of the Ryot to whom
" the plant belongs, and the name of the boat-manjee, or
" hackeryman who brought it to the factory, are likewise
" written. Each Ryot has the date and number of bun-
" dles entered on a separate paper, which he retains:
" this is called a *haat chitty*. The *haat chitty* is brought
" whenever its owner brings plant, and the entries are
" duly made day by day, agreeing, of course, with those
" in the *amdánni*, the book in which all the plant is en-
" tered, and which is written in duplicate. When the
" measurement of the plant is finished, one book is taken
" to the superintendent, or, if there is none at the factory,
" it is sent to that at which he resides, and the other
" remains in the *sherishta*. Any one who has seen the
" confusion in a *neel cola* when two or three hundred
" Ryots are delivering plant, will allow that the mohurrir
" cannot conveniently make false entries at that time.
" The *haat chitty*, and the *amdánni* are checks one on
" the other; the duplicate *amdánni* is a check on both;
" for the Ryot is quite as willing to connive with the
" mohurrir to cheat the planter, as the mohurrir may be
" to cheat either one or the other. When the manufac-
" turing is finished, the entries are written in a book,
" which is to the *amdánni* what the ledger is to the daily
" cash-book. There is a page for each Ryot, which
" shews the dates on which he brought plant, and the
" quantity. This being done, the Ryots are called in
" to settle their accounts, and which, *haat chitties* in
" hand, they do. This is the plan pursued, and it ap-
" pears one calculated to protect the Ryot far more than
" the planter."

Every thing seems here to be done to give the culti-

vator his due. Of course the natives will cheat, and
bribe, and quarrel, and bring false accusations against
each other. Many judges have reported it as a general
proposition, that all accusations made by the police are
inventions, with no other end than extortion. The planter
cannot say much more for his native servants than that
they are better looked after than the police, and are not
so shamelessly corrupt as the judges' omlah. We are
not claiming for the planter that he is a beneficent deity :
we only assert of him that he is an honest man, doing
his best in a corrupt state of society, and doing better
than the Government does.

What we have to add to this statement of the relations
of the planters and the Ryots will be by way of admissions, and we will make them as frankly and unreservedly
as if we were stating the strongest facts in favour of the
cause for which we are seeking a hearing.

Among the institutions which the British settler found
in force in the interior were many jurisdictions analogous
to those feudal rights once common in Europe.* The
Zemindar was the lord of the manor. He had the power
to summon his tenants to his courts, just as our lords of
the manor had the power to summon their copyhold or
freehold tenants to their manor courts to perform suit and
service.† He had armed retainers, whom he employed to

---

* In an article in the *Calcutta Review* for June 1847, Mr. Seton
Karr, who drew up the Indigo Report, 1860, but had not then the
influence of Mr. Grant so strong upon him, says—

" To the *Zemindars* is due the invention of the lattial system. We
" can affirm with the fullest confidence that it was not the device of the
" planter; that, left to himself, and with the prospect of fair dealing
" and speedy justice, he would not thus have taken up arms in broad
" daylight."

† This has been taken away by special act of the Legislature, directed
against the "interlopers," but most grievously felt by the Zemindars,

guard him from robbers, and to serve him in his quarrels, or, under the name of lattials, or stick-men, to punish his Ryots. All these privileges he used against the settler, to make his Ryots refuse to grow indigo or to make them grow it, according as the settler propitiated him or set him at defiance. He also used his lattials to destroy or cut the patches of indigo for which the settler had advanced money. Of course the settler was not long in following this custom. He also hired a set of lattials for his own protection, and to neutralize the lattials of the bludgeon-men, and in trials of stick-play the Europeans soon got the better. In Kishnaghur and in all the indigo districts all this is quite gone out of fashion since the planters have leased the Zemindars' feudal rights. Even thirteen years ago Mr. Seton Karr referred to it as " A Tale of the Past." At the present moment he and Mr. Grant, in the " Minute" and in the " Report," only insinuate the descent of these historic irregularities. They talk of lattials in Jessore just as a demagogue inveighing against monarchy might talk of ship-money in Buckinghamshire.

So, also, the planter holding manors (or Zemindaries), by " putnee" or permanent lease had succeeded to the reputed right of summoning the Ryot to pay his rent, and make up his indigo account ; and it must be admitted that, whether the planter has or has not the lease of the manor, he had at one time come to usurp this right, and to summon the Ryots to the house to make up his accounts.

This is what Mr. Grant calls " kidnapping." It is an

whom it has crippled in their power of collecting their (and the Government's) rents. Government, however, retains its powers of selling and buying in, the whole Zemindary upon an instant's delay.

old Native practice.   It is just as if an English landowner sent out and made his farmers come to his audit,
with this exception, that an English farmer neither requires or would submit to any such compulsion, and the
Bengali is used to it from time immemorial.   But let us
suppose that there was in England no remedy by distress,
no County Court, no Civil Assizes, no other remedy
but a Chancery suit to recover the rent or arrears of
a thousand small tenants—in fact no law at all—should
we not, think you, have lattials and "kidnapping" in
England?

These "kidnappings," when rare instances do occur,
are a disgrace, not to the planters, but to Mr. Grant and
his class.   Is it not monstrous, under a civilized Government, that a vast industry and a great class of capitalists
should be so outlawed that they should be driven, in extreme cases, to do for themselves what the Government
of the country ought to do for them?   Is it not a scandal
that the planter has not the facility which the meanest
English "tallyman" has, that of summoning his debtor
before an honest unsuspected rural judge, and making
him make up his accounts, or perform his contract?   If
it was not for the fact that a planter is one white man
dwelling among 200,000 natives, the wonder would be,
not that now and then, a planter, under the sting of
some aggravating fraud, is found to right himself, but
that the law of the Mofussil is not habitually a rule of
violence.   Such a system could only have been deliberately invented in order to produce violence, and to com-
pass the traditional policy of the East-India Company
and their "pucka civilians."   Mr. Grant, when he manufactures his sneers out of stories a quarter of a century
old, and recollects what short work he makes with his

own salt and opium Ryots, must wonder in his secret soul how the planters could have withstood the pressure he and his friends have put upon them for years long past.

However, to account for an evil is not to justify it. There is no country where any violence is so much to be deprecated as in India, for the execution must be delegated to natives, who will be certain to conduct it in the worst manner. With a trustworthy police, independent judges, and a simple law, nothing of the sort ever would occur. Such cases are, indeed, exceedingly rare. Mr. Grant is obliged to recur to his imagination, or his Indian traditions, when he wants a modern instance. But if the number were a thousand times greater, the remedy is in the hands of Mr. Grant. He has only to establish efficient small-contract Courts in India, and to allow justice to take her course unterrified and unchecked, and the Ryot would have immediate remedy against the planter, and the planter against the Ryot. There is not the least reason why, if public disturbers, like this Lieutenant-Governor of Bengal, were kept from intermeddling, or were never trusted with public stations, and if the blessing of cheap and speedy justice were distributed in India, as it is in England,—there is no reason, we say, why an indigo plantation should not be as happy and peaceful as a model English parish, with a resident landlord and an attentive clergyman.*

* Of course this assertion supposes that the peace of the country is kept, and equal protection is given by Government to all classes. We are not pretending that the antagonism of race will lie dormant in the case of indigo, or cotton, or tea, or silk, any more than in the case of Zillah Judges.

. How long would the civilians be safe in the Mofussil if some superior power could say to the Zemindars and Ryots—"don't obey the authorities, we will protect you?" How long would the Missionaries

Such have been, in times immediately antecedent to the accession of the present Lieutenant-Governor of Bengal, the dealings between the capitalist and the native labourer in Bengal. When the mutinies broke out, the good relations of the Ryots and indigo planters were very manifest. One of the conspicuous facts of the great mutiny was the defence by Mr. Venables, the indigo planter, of the district of Azimghur, after the Civil servants had all run away.* It was the good understanding kept up by the indigo planters with the natives at Baraset which enabled Mr. Eden to hold his ground there, giving him intelligence of a conspiracy to murder him, and enabling him later to indulge in the luxury of an exemplary ingratitude, by exciting a social *jaquerie* among the indigo planters' debtors. It is a fact worth a thousand of Mr. Grant's inuendoes, or his Secretary, Mr. Seton Karr's, astute insinuations, that during the time when the Company's native judges were trying and sentencing Queen's officers and Company's servants, no indigo planter was

remain in India if they were not backed and protected by British bayonets? The planters being now deserted by those who hold the bayonets at their command, are, as a matter of course, thrown into the power of a hostile race, who hate civilian, missionary, and planter in an equal degree, or perhaps the missionary the most and the planter the least. The mutiny gives conclusive evidence of the hatred borne by natives to all Europeans or indeed Christians—surely it is a very suicidal policy for one set of Englishmen to ruin another in a foreign country, and even the thinking portion of the natives must laugh at the house divided against itself, and be full of hope that their time is coming to gain the ascendancy, when they see Mr. Grant at his work.

* Very few of the Tirhoot planters did leave the district, and very few were even warned to leave.

When the Tirhoot planters were warned by the civilians to leave the district, they made over their factories to their native head-men, and on their return, they found the work had gone on steadily during their absence. This is another fact to shew the relation between planter and Ryot, when the civilians do not interfere.

murdered, or even harmed. This fact has sunk deep into the minds of the British people, and even into the minds of the present generation of Civil servants. The fact realized all that Metcalfe and Bentinck had foretold, and there are now plenty of civilians to admit, even in their official reports, that if British settlers had been encouraged in India there would have been no rebellion.* Every thing is subdued to the new reign of common sense, and the postponement of class jealousies to the imperial good, *præter atrocem animum Catonis.* Grant, and his little surrounding of Civil lattials, are as they ever were; or even as J. Jebb and J. Pattison were, when expostulating with George Canning against allowing Englishmen to go to India.

So much for the normal relation of the planter and the Ryots.

* Wherever there were British settlers in any number, viz. : Sarun, Champarun, Tirhoot, and Lower Bengal, there was no rebellion.

CHAPTER VI.

THE RELATIONS OF THE GOVERNMENT TO THEIR RYOTS.

A FEW words as to opium. Mr. Grant forces us to allude to it, in order to demonstrate that his conduct to us is not an honest error, or a delusion that he is benefiting the Ryot when he ruins his employers. The most suspicious reader of this address will scarcely believe in any pretences to philanthropic motives which Mr. Grant may put forth, when he sees the character of the opium labour which Mr. Grant in his official capacity enforces, and compares it with that which Mr. Grant has interfered to destroy.

We do not labour the subject, because we are quite sensible to the fact, that if indigo could be proved to be a pernicious cultivation, we should not justify its culture by proving that opium is *more* pernicious.

But we are charging conduct against Mr. Grant and those immediate subordinates whose acts he controls and rewards, which, in our judgment, possibly prejudiced in such a matter, can only be explained by a deliberate intention to ruin every independent British interest in India, and to consummate the old traditionary policy of extruding all interlopers from India.

We mention this word opium, then, not to justify the culture of indigo, for no one dreams that a harmless dye, employing labour, clearing the jungle, and spreading annually millions of capital over the rural districts of Bengal, needs any justification; but in order to shew the impossibility that a man can be honest when he pretends that he can see "forced labour" in the indigo factory, while he is himself the controller and director of the Government opium works. To the man who, with the beam in his own eye, sought to pluck out the mote in his brother's eye, the apostrophe was, "Thou hypocrite!"

A few words, therefore, about opium.

In the first place, no person within the Bengal territories is allowed to grow the poppy, except on Government account.

Annual engagements are entered into by the cultivators, under a system of pecuniary advances to sow a certain quantity of land with the poppy; and the whole produce, in the form of opium, is delivered to the Government at a fixed rate.

Opium requires the richest land. No crop in India requires so much care and labour as the cultivation of the poppy. The ground has to be ploughed six or eight times, harrowed, well-manured, and watered. It was (Colebrooke in his Husbandry of Bengal states) an unprofitable crop for the Ryots, who were, however, tempted to engage in it "only in consequence of the advances made by the Government agents." The poppy is a delicate plant, peculiarly liable to injury from insects, wind, hail, or unseasonable rain. "The produce" (Colebrooke says) "runs in extremes: while one cultivator is disap-
" pointed, another reaps immense gain: one season does
" not pay the labour of culture—another, peculiarly for-
" tunate, enriches all the cultivators."

The contracts for the cultivation are entered into with the Ryots in August or September, when the Ryots receive their advance from the Government of four rupees per beegah. The sowings commence in November. The crop is collected in March or April, when the account with the Ryot is finally settled, on each man's produce being delivered and weighed.

The fixed price given to the Ryot is 3s 6d, or 1 rupee 12 annas for every pound of manufactured opium delivered to the Government agent : at least, the above was, for many years, the fixed price; but a year ago the cultivation fell off so much, that Government had to make an advance to the Ryot of a few half-pence per pound on the fixed rate.

When opium sells at 900 rupees per chest, it gives the Government equal to . . . 11s 0d per pound.
Deduct from this paid to the Ryot, 3s 6d
_____

Leaving for the Government . 7s 6d per pound.

But for some time past opium has been selling at nearer 1800 rupees per chest, or double the above price, which gives to the Government, say 22s 0d per pound.
Deduct from this paid to the Ryot, 3s 6d
_____

Leaving for the Government, 18s 6d per pound, or 600 per cent. upon the cost price of the opium.

No interest or commission is charged on the advances made to the Ryots. The account of one season must be settled before the commencement of the next, and no outstanding balance is allowed to stand over.

If the cultivator neglect to bring sufficient produce to cover his advance, *the balance is at once recovered by legal means, by a summary process applicable to opium cases alone.*

As to the manner in which the opium Ryots are compelled to accept the advances, we may cite, for the public

opinion on the subject, the official letter of Mr. Farquharson, the opium agent of Behar. He reports that,

" 23. The newspapers were at one time full of stories
of the compulsory and oppressive nature of the opium
cultivation. Gentlemen travelling dâk heard from their
bearers stories of money being thrown, as opium advances,
into Ryots' houses, and the Ryots thereby bound to cultivate countless fields of poppy at a ruinous loss to themselves, and that on refusal. or remonstrance, they were
seized and carried off to the opium cutcherries, and confined and beaten till their recusance was overcome."

Of course Mr. Farquharson insists that the travellers
had been " imposed upon," and Mr. Grant doubtless is
incredulous as to these stories. Yet there are many very
credible Europeans who can prove the facts just as the
newspapers stated them. Mr. Grant seems to have read
and believed these statements, substituting " indigo " for
" opium."

Mr. Farquharson applied to the Rev. L. F. Kalberer
to corroborate his report as to his view that the opium
Ryots are not, as stated, ground to the earth by fiscal
oppression and by countless hosts of Government spies.
The reverend gentleman answered the appeal, but rather
faintly, and from his favourable testimony we are able to
extract the following rather damnatory points in the
evidence of a witness called to exculpate. He says—we
take the admissions and omit the reverend gentleman's
exculpatory evidence—

" There may be spies in the Abkaree Department in
large towns. I have heard of such a thing, but am not
certain of the facts, that the Ryots should not smuggle it;
if there are, notwithstanding it is smuggled, which enables
the poorer class to eat it.

" I may here be allowed to subjoin some common conversations which we often had with the Ryots, as they often have sat with us for hours, and naturally religious conversations are first, but others are also introduced, for instance : —

" Why do you sow opium?—Because it enables me to pay my land rent and do other business with the money as we get advance, which is very convenient.

" Do you sow it willingly?—Because the Government wishes us to do so.

" Are you compelled to sow it?—Yes.

" By whom?—By the Zemindar, and sometimes by the *Zillahdar.*

" Why?—He gets his land rent easily, and is profitable to him.

" But can you not give it up when you like?—Yes, but I do not like to give it up, because the advances are very convenient, and we have not to pay interest of that money.

" Are you compelled to sow opium?—Yes.

Others again—

" If you were not, would you not sow ?—No.

" Last February we were at Gya, one of our cartmen's brother became our watchman; often these men praised their Zemindar very much for his kindness and care of his Ryots,—a very rare thing. Some years ago he ordered all his Ryots of about twenty villages to cease opium cultivation ; they obeyed his order."

Such is the evidence obtained by an *opium agent* seeking for testimony *in favour* of his masters. Is it not even stronger than any evidence that Mr. Grant has been able to obtain by a Commission seeking evidence *against* the indigo planter? Mr. Grant's own evidence

in favour of his opium is more damnatory to himself
than his hostile and thoroughly contradicted evidence
against indigo is inimical to the system of indigo cultivation. Yet he professes to proclaim the country against
the indigo manufacturer in the interest of the native?
We ask again, is it possible that this can be an honest
delusion?

While we are upon this matter of forced purchase by
Government under a system of summary punishments, we
ought also to say something upon

SALT.

In Bengal the manufacture of salt is carried on, on
account of the Government by the system of pecuniary
advances; the parties advanced to being bound to deliver,
at a fixed price, all the salt manufactured. The salt in
Bengal is obtained by boiling the sea-water. The manufacturers are called Molungees : about 100,000 of them
are engaged on the Sunderbunds near Calcutta.

The average cost of production is 80 rupees per 100
maunds, or something under one farthing per pound,
while the Government sells it at an average of one penny
per pound.

The native salt agents were accused of being great
oppressors of the Molungees, who were cheated in the
weight delivered : and being reported to be short of the delivery contracted for, the native agent made the conceal-
ment of this a farther ground of extortion. The native
agent next makes use of the unfortunate Molungee as the
medium of selling the concealed salt to the smugglers.

Interest was charged to him upon the advance. Once

on the wrong side, he seldom got again on the right one :
he became a bondsman for life when once indebted ; and
every Molungee so situated was made to believe that his
children's children were bound for his debt to the Government. The native agents were responsible for keeping
a sharp look out upon these Molungees ; but many of
them managed, notwithstanding, to make their escape,
indebted to the Government. The custom was for the
native agent to screen himself by reporting to Government that all those who ran away had been carried
off by tigers.

There is not quite the same oppression now, the native
agents being better looked after ; but, notwithstanding
this the Molungees, or salt manufacturers, are looked upon
as the poorest class of labourers in all Bengal, much
worse off than the Ryots under the most tyrannical
indigo planter of those old times when the Company
managed to keep all out of the Mofussil but the most
reckless adventurers who had fled from shipboard.

Of late years opium figures at about five millions, and
salt at about two millions sterling, in the revenue of the
Indian Government.

This matter of the Government Ryot and the planters'
Ryot has recently been very well treated by the *Calcutta
Englishman*, in dealing with the Indigo Report, 1860.
This newspaper says—

" One of the charges brought against the planters is
their neglect of observing the change taking place around
them, the rise in value of all produce, whilst they did not
pay the Ryots for the produce in proportion. The Indigo
Commission report on this subject, and state it as a primary cause of the dislike of the Ryot to the cultivation.

We looked into the papers before us for any recognition on the part of the Government of these same signs of the times, and to discover if they had done justice to their Ryots by giving them an advance in proportion to the rise in price of produce. We know that Government very tardily raised the price of opium to the Ryots in Tirhoot, but we wished more particularly to see what had been done in the same country where the indigo Ryots had revolted against the low rates paid them by the planters. The Government then have not raised the rates *paid to their Molungees, or salt Ryots, one fraction beyond what they paid five years ago—rise in price of rice notwithstanding.* The value of land has risen, of labour has risen, and of 'indigo plant has risen, but no rise has taken place to the Molungee."

" At Hidgelle the amount paid by Government to the Molungee in 1850 *was six annas* [ninepence] *per maund* (of eighty-four lbs.), and the same rate continues up to 1860, seven annas being paid to one division and six annas in the other. At Tumlook we have the same thing: in 1850 the price paid is seven annas, and from 1857 a small rise by quarters of an anna yearly up to 1860, when the price remained at eight annas per maund. If we are to consider this as an advance of price of about fourteen per cent., *still it is nothing to the advance the planters have made in the same period of time.* There is nothing more clearly shews the injustice of the Bengal Government to the planters than the statements here given of their conduct towards their own Ryots. A perwanna issued in the salt districts, stating that the Molungees were not bound to manufacture salt unless they pleased, and that they could only be prosecuted in the Civil

Courts, would raise a disturbance quite equal to that which has occurred in Bengal, if not greater."*

* To avoid this disagreeable comparison, and, let us hope, in order to save these poor creatures from actual starvation, after which they could produce no salt, Mr. Grant, it is said, is now about to raise the rates of the salt Ryots. We would even "willingly believe" that the Lieutenant-Governor had been influenced "by the compassion, the sincerity, and the kindness of a Christian," if he had not expended his Christian virtue upon exciting idleness among the indigo Ryots, while his own salt Ryots were starving.

CHAPTER VII.

In 1859, after the extinction of the rebellion, and perhaps owing to the English capital therein expended, there was a general rise throughout Bengal of the prices of labour and rice.

What happens in England when corn goes down to a very low rate? All the small leaseholders get suddenly dissatisfied. It is no longer the little, normal matters of dispute, such as letting the gates and homesteads get out of repair, selling off hay, and bringing on no manure, growing more than the two regular successive straw crops. The English landowner has his little regular difficulties of this sort, just like the Indian planter in his quiet times. But when corn gets very low, the discontents of these little farmers of arable farms get serious. They talk, perhaps without much meaning, of throwing up their leases; and they sometimes let the rent run in arrear. Above all, they cast a covetous eye upon the meadowland and the pasture-land down by the river, when they mark the contrast between the high price of meat and the low price of corn.

This was just the case with the Ryots in 1859. There had been, as Mr. Larmour shewed the Calcutta Commission the other day, several years of disastrous failure in the indigo crops, while the rice crops had been thriving; and the Ryots had got into arrears with the planter, and

F

did not like the crop they were under contract to cultivate. It was a critical condition of affairs, and especially under a Government which has no available law of
contracts.

In the ordinary course of things, however, the difficulty
must have soon blown over. There would have been a
great deal of talk, and, after some delay, the planters
would have seen, as they have seen upon five former occasions, that some concession must be made : and it would
have been made. Our English plan in such case is to
return a per centage for one year. That would not do in
India, where all is paid in advance, even to the chickens
which are to come when the sitting hen has hatched
them,* and where nothing that is once given can be taken
back. The planter would have advanced the price a little ;
he would have agreed to carry the plant to the factory :
one or two average seasons would have brought the Ryots
up even with the factory, as we have already seen happened to Mr. Larmour's Ryots, and matters would have
jogged on again in their usual way.

"My Ryots," (said Mr. Larmour,) " have always
" worked with me freely and cheerfully, and unless, when
" misled or instigated against me, as in the present sea-
" son, they have always been glad to meet me when I
" visited their villages, and to point out with pride their
" indigo cultivation."

Unhappily, however, there was at Baraset one of those
very energetic civilians in whose eyes the planter, but
especially the planter's cutcherry, is an abomination. The
planter, in his arbitration court, has more than all the crimes
laid to his charge which Shylock alleged against Antonio.

* Mr. Larmour's Evidence before Indigo Commission, 1860.

Not only does he lend money without usury, but he does justice between the Ryots in their own quarrels, *without taking fees or consuming stamps,* and by his illegal and voluntary court of arbitration, he diminishes the importance and the supremacy of such civilians as Mr. Eden. Now was the time to send a shot right between wind and water into the whole class of such interlopers.

Mr. Eden at once took advantage of this happy opportunity, and, as magistrate of Baraset, he, on the 17th August, 1859, wrote a letter to his native deputy-magistrate, "for his information and guidance." He called to his attention that "the Ryot is at liberty to sow any crop he likes," and that "where contracts or promises may be admitted, there may still be many irresistible pleas to avoid the consequences the planters insist upon."

Imagine the effect of a magistrate volunteering this false and dishonest counsel to an excited and discontented population, already trying to force the planters out of their contracts. Was any more execrable advice ever given? Will the reader of these pages believe that a magistrate, a Christian man, and English gentleman, could publicly inform a population of pagans that although their contracts or promises might be undeniable, yet they were not bound by their promise or contract, but were at liberty to sow any crop they liked? We laugh to scorn Mr. Eden's subterfuge, as to whether the contracts had or had not a clause of right of entry. This was what he intended the Ryots to understand, what he knew the Ryots would understand, and what the Ryots did understand—namely, that the Government wished the indigo contracts to be thrown up and the indigo manufacture abolished.

The native deputy-magistrate naturally turned this

F 2

letter into a proclamation, and posted it all over the district of Baraset.*

We should seek in vain for any parallel case in this country. If some frenzy had seized the British farmers

---

* This is the letter:—

"To BABOO HEMCHUNDER KUR,

"*Depy. Magistrate Kalarooah Sub-Division.*

"SIR,—As the cultivation of indigo is carried on to a considerable extent in your sub-division, I beg to forward you, for your information and guidance, extracts from a letter, No. 4516, dated 21st July 1859, from the Secretary to the Government of Bengal to the Commissioner of the Nuddea Division.

"You will perceive that the course laid down for the police in indigo disputes is to protect the Ryot in the possession of his lands, on which he is at liberty to sow any crop he likes, without any interference on the part of the planter or any one else. The planter is not at liberty, under pretext of the Ryot having promised to sow indigo for him, to enter forcibly upon the land of the Ryot. Such promises can only be produced against the Ryot in the Civil Court, and the magisterial authority have nothing to do with them, for there must be two parties to a promise, and it is possible that the Ryots, whose promises or contracts are admitted, may still have many irresistible pleas to avoid the consequence the planter insists upon."

This is the proclamation :—

"*Translation.*

"To the Darogah of Thannah Kalarooah. Take notice.—A letter from the Magistrate of Baraset, dated the 17th August, 1859, having been received, accompanied by an extract from an English letter from the Secretary to the Government of Bengal, to the address of the Commissioner of the Nuddea Division, dated 21st July, 1859, No. 4516, to the following purport, that in cases of disputes relating to indigo Ryots they shall retain possession of their own lands, and shall sow in them what crops they please, and the police will be careful that no indigo planter nor any one else be able to interfere in the matter, and indigo planters shall not be able forcibly to cause indigo to be sown on the lands of those Ryots on the ground that the Ryots consented to the sowing, &c., of indigo. If Ryots have so consented, the indigo planter may bring an action against them in the Civil Court. The Criminal Court has no concern in these matters, because, *notwithstanding such contracts, or such consent withheld or given, Ryots may urge unanswerable excuses against the sowing of indigo.* A copy of perwannah is therefore issued, and you are requested in future to act accordingly.— Dated 20th August, 1859."

to grow no more straw crops until protection had been
restored, and a Conservative ministry—we beg pardon of
that great party for so injurious a supposition—were to
issue a proclamation, setting forth that the farmers would
be protected by the whole force of the police in carrying
out their project, and reminding the magistrates that there
was no remedy to make them sow except a suit in Chancery for specific performance of their agreements, which
of course was, as against thousands of farmers, inopera-
tive ;—if such a proclamation as this had been put forth,
at a moment when the people were excited by causes
arising from the fluctuation of prices, might it not even
in England have produced a very frightful disaster? and
can there be any doubt that when the nation returned to
its senses the madmen who had so misused their power
would be impeached?   But even this violent supposition
can give no idea of the consequences of such a document
as we have just set forth, disseminated in a country accustomed to despotic institutions: among a race habituated
to look up to the Government as the irresistible and un-
appeasable tyrant before whom even the white settlers are
but dust, and at whose breath licenses are recalled,
planters disappear from their places, and districts of re-
claimed jungle go back to bulrushes.   The subtle Asiatic
mind is always ready to jump at a meaning beyond what
is expressed in the rough language of the crass Western.
But if the Bengali had scanned it never so closely, what
could he have made out of this proclamation, except that
the " Sircar" had determined to turn the Europeans out
of the Mofussil, and were desirous that no more indigo
should be sown?   Hedge it around with what nice distinctions you may, if you come down to an excited class
of cultivators under agreements to sow, and volunteer to

them a promise that they shall sow what they like, and that, as to their agreements, they can only be enforced in the Civil Courts, and that many irresistible pleas may set them aside even when admitted—what can a native understand from this, except that you wish to put an end to indigo; and that he is not only emancipated from his agreements, but that it will offend the Government, and do no good to any one, even if he should carry them out.*

.

* Mr. Larmour's evidence upon this subject is as follows :—

Mr. Seton Karr.] Q. You are aware that a dislike to the cultivation of indigo has been generally manifested in some districts this spring, and that in some concerns the Ryots distinctly refuse to sow in spite of persuasion, and with the consequences of the summary law (passed for six months, and now expired) before them : will you give the Commission your opinion as to the causes of this dislike and mutiny?

A. The present spirit of the Ryots, especially in the district of Kishnaghur, has been caused, in the first instance, by a perwannah issued by the Magistrate of Baraset, telling the Ryots of that concern that they were at liberty to sow indigo or not, and if the planter attempted to enforce it, he must have recourse to the Civil Court. The effect of such perwannah could only have been construed into the meaning that it was the Magistrate's wish that the Ryots should not sow indigo, and the effect of this perwannah was that the Ryots not only refused to sow indigo, but they did not pay their rents. This perwannah was again followed up by the Magistrate of Baraset sending extracts of a letter from the Lieutenant-Governor of Bengal to Mr. Grote, Commissioner of the Nuddea division, which extracts were translated into Bengali, and a perwannah *sent round to the thannahs of the sub-division of Kullarooa, telling the Ryots again that they were at liberty to sow indigo, or not, as it suited them. These perwannahs had the effect of rousing all the Ryots throughout the Kishnaghur district, and inducing them to attempt to break their engagements. These perwannahs were followed up by a letter from the Secretary to Government of Bengal to the Commissioner of the Nuddea division, finding fault with the conduct of the Magistrate and Deputy Magistrate of Nuddea, in cases in which indigo planters were concerned, and which led the natives generally to believe that the Lieutenant-Governor of Bengal was strongly prejudiced against indigo and indigo planting.* The Ryots, labouring under the belief that they would receive the support of Government in not fulfilling their engagements, beame very daring, and *attacked and maltreated Europeans when riding about the country.* A petition was presented through the Commissioner of Nuddea by myself, dated 4th February last, begging for the immediate interference of Government to counteract the impres-

Tell any class of men that they may pay their debts or not as they please, and what would be the consequence? Is it possible that we have to argue this before an impartial public, and that firebrands who have, for wantonness, or vanity, or *esprit de corps*, put such tremendous interests at peril, should be retained in posts of authority by a rational people? At the cost of how many millions do the people of England think they keep this Mr. Eden in office? How many rebellions, and the loss of how many millions of trade, shall we cheerfully undergo for the pleasure of having Mr. J. P. Grant's favorite in power in Bengal?

No sooner had these perwannahs issued, than, gradually and surely, the word passed through the plains, that, in the words of Mr. Larmour, " Government was determined to crush all European interest in the country." The consequences were not doubtful. It is not only the Bengali who will kick the falling. The natives laughed at their arrears, as they were much in the habit of doing, but they also laughed at their agreements for the coming season. The feeling began to grow. Europeans, as they rode about, were insulted, and a little more delay, and Mr. Eden's proclamation would be followed out by a murder or two. A petition to the Government met with no attention whatever. There was a *jaquerie* rising. Mr. Eden had gaily raised it, but Government probably never opened the despatches which announced it. It was a very light matter for Mr. Eden—a mere rustic rising, quite harmless to Mr. Eden, with his fortified gaol and his

sion that the Ryots had received from the reports that had been circulated, and the perwannahs that had been issued. *No notice whatever was taken of my representation,* and when a notification was issued to disabuse the Ryots' minds, it came too late, and had no good effect."

armed guard; but very unpleasant to planters dwelling alone in open houses, and with a population about
them impressed with the belief that Government wanted to
get rid of the interlopers once for all, and that their factories might be had for the sacking.   More wonderful
even than the safety of the planters during the mutinies
is the fact that the Ryots resisted this temptation as
they did.

This is the sort of excitable people, ready to believe that
even a dog in high office must be inspired, whom Mr.
Eden, at a. critical moment, let loose upon the indigo
planters of Bengal.   That nothing should be wanting to
keep up the belief of the people, fast and furious came
missives to the same purpose.   There were letters from the
Secretary of Government, in the Eden vein.   The storm
was beginning to howl.   Magistrates and Civil servants
in the neighbourhood, men who knew the districts and the
magnitude of the impending peril, were censured, or removed, because they dared to report against Mr. Eden's
proceedings.   Sir F. Halliday had, unhappily, at that
moment been succeeded by Mr. J. P. Grant, as Lieutenant-Governor of Bengal.

Mr. Eden's perwannahs were issued on the 20th of
August 1859, and had been immediately made the object
of loud remonstrance.

The Commissioner, Mr. Grote, an officer of great experience and judgment, saw at once the danger of these
proclamations; and being Mr. Eden's immediate superior,
he condemned his conduct and reversed his decisions.
Mr. Eden appealed to the Lieutenant-Governor of
Bengal.

The Lieutenant-Governor took time enough for deliberation, and on the 7th April, 1860, Mr. J. P. Grant

condescended to say that he was of opinion that Mr.
Eden had given a satisfactory explanation.

A few days previous to this last date, Mr. Grant,
jealous of the laurels of his subordinate, had published,
as a Government document, a letter from himself to Mr.
Sconce, containing this sentence :—

"I am myself of opinion that the indigo cultivators"
(meaning the Ryots) "have and long have had great and
increasing ground of just complaint against the whole
system of indigo cultivation."

The planters have nothing to do with Mr. Grant's opinion. But whatever may be a man's prejudices, whether
he be opium manufacturer or not, no honest man could
read the papers in Mr. Grant's own office, or even the
small part we have quoted, nor could he even hold his ears
open to notorious facts, and say, whatever may be "the
grounds of complaint against the whole system of indigo
cultivation," that those "grounds of complaint" are now
"upon the increase." Every man, however, has a right
to his opinion, sensate, or insensate. What we denounce
as an atrocious act, tending directly to confusion and
bloodshed, is the publication of this "opinion," without inquiry and without jurisdiction, at such a moment as this,
when the whole trade, and the capital of that trade, and
perhaps, also, the lives of the British settlers, and the
peace of the country, hung upon a thread.

What, we ask the people of England, who will certainly
have to pay for all wars which their officials may wantonly provoke—what could be the object of a man who,
with his salt Ryots starving on one side of him, and his
opium Ryots driven to their forced labour on the other
side, turns to the indigo Ryots, with whom he has no
official connexion whatever, and advises them to oppose

" the whole system of indigo culture ?" Can we assign
it to any other motive than a design to extirpate the indigo planter from India ?

The planters then went up to the Legislative Council,
and stated the urgency of the danger; and the Council
recognised that urgency. The planters asked a very
simple boon. They only desired a temporary measure
giving a summary remedy to enforce existing indigo contracts. It was not wanted to put Ryots in prison, and
it was to a very slight degree put in force; but it was
wanted as an authentic declaration of the Government of
the country against those two great official agitators, Mr.
Eden and Mr. Grant. It was wanted as a counter proclamation to the perwannahs of Baraset. It was wanted
as a disavowal of Mr. Grant's proscription of the indigo
culture, and of the Hon. Ashley Eden's " satisfactorily
explained" perwannahs.

For the poison was brewing, and from that time to
this it has gone on spreading and infecting the whole
population of Bengal. Almost every day since his first
sweeping denunciation of the indigo manufacture, Mr.
Grant has been able to publish some new manifestation
of discontent and disorder in the Mofussil. The strange
thing is, that the man actually seems to think that these
crimes, which are as much his own as if he committed
them with his own hands, are rather feathers in his cap.
He has nursed up a rebellion, and he is now twitting the
planters with the dangers they run, after he has hallooed
the natives upon them. It is quite true that, under the
presumed protection of Mr. Grant, the Ryots will not
work out their advances, and are looting the factories,
and ill-treating the planters; in some instances threatening their lives, and very generally refusing to pay to Mr.

Grant's enemies even their RENT.* The last phase of
Mr. Grant's *jaquerie* is that the Ryots have got to the
point of refusing to pay rents to native Zemindars as
well as planters.

This is a pleasant spirit to have conjured up just as

* See the official Report of Mr. Reid, the Commissioner for Rajshahye
division. It must sound to Mr. Grant like a song of victory.

" It is to the next sowing season, now imminent, that the most earnest attention of the authorities must now be directed. The Ryots of
most of the concerns in Pubna have expressed their determination not
to sow any more indigo, and where the planter is also Zemindar, they
*have now proceeded, in some parts, to attempt to avoid the punctual
payment of their rents* by offering to deposit them with the collector.
Their *avowed* reason is to avoid having to pay unauthorised cesses, but
the real reason, I believe, is, that they may be enabled to break off all
connection whatsoever with the factory.

" The magistrate reports that there is a very strong combination
amongst the Ryots to break off their connection with indigo, and that
one Mohesh Chunder Bundopodhya, an inhabitant of the Nuddea district, is the prime mover in it. The Ryots are much excited, and,
although perhaps not intentionally seeking to break the peace, a breach
of it may, I concur with the magistrate in thinking, be brought about
at any moment by an accidental collision. Every endeavour must be
made to prevent this occurring, and measures have been taken to bind
down Mohesh Chunder Bundopodhya who, there seems strong grounds
to suppose, will incite a rupture.

" Mr. Hampton, of Salgamodia, has already been *bound down* (*!!!*)
together with his factory Naib. Mr. Hampton is the manager of Mr.
Kenny's factories, the excitement in which is far greater than elsewhere.
He assured me that it was his intention to abstain most carefully from
doing any thing which might lead to a rupture. He expressed a fear,
at the same time that, *not only would the factories be closed, but also
that he would be unable to collect his rents, and that his estates would
be brought to the hammer.*"

The consummation of this last expectation would make Mr. Grant's
work very complete. If Mr. Grant can stop the payment of rents, the
game is his own. If the planter cannot gather his rents he cannot pay
the Government, and there is no difficulty of civil forms about *their*
remedies. They sell the whole property at once for what it will fetch :
the old plan was to sell it at about one-hundredth part of its value, and
buy it up for the Company. Mr. Grant may intend to use this traditional device, and to sell up the planters, as his predecessors sold up
the old princes of India.

the Government is going into these districts to collect *Income Tax !*

Yet the Lieut.-Governor actually luxuriates in this. Here is a letter just published by the Government in Calcutta. It is a picture of the interior. The Lieut.-Governor here shews us how the Bengali pranks, when Mr. Grant has relieved him from all his obligations and all his duties. The letter is from Mr. E. Roberts, of Commercolly, to the assistant magistrate of that station. It details the experience of an exceedingly respectable planter during these disturbances; but the odd thing is that Mr. Grant should publish it.

"In the month of July last," says Mr. Roberts, "an influential Jotedar of Mirzapore village, named Harran Joadar, forcibly took away some 'paddy' belonging to one Baramdy Sheik of Durrumparah, who complained to me. I advised him to institute a case against Joadar in the Fouzdarree Court at Commercolly, which he did. I gave the man what assistance I could, and desired my Mooktear to look after his rights in Court. After the complaint was lodged, Harran Joadar came to me at Benepore, and requested me to force Baramdy to 'rajeenama' the case. I refused, and the next day the work of Benepore factory was very nearly stopped by the influence of Harran, who induced the Ryots not to cut indigo. Seeing this, and rather than that Messrs. Wm. Moran and Company should lose their fine crop of indigo, I so far yielded to the wishes of Joadar, that I withdrew my support from Baramdy. Very soon afterwards, the latter was intimidated by the former into withdrawing the suit.

"Seeing the success of Harran Joadar, one Habizoollah Kazee of Kachakole village, who had long had his eye on a jummá belonging to one Oofatoollah, requested me to take it forcibly from its rightful owner, and to give it to him (Habizoollah).   I refused, and again my Bene-pore factory was on the point of being closed by the machinations of Harran Joadar and Habizoollah.   My fair and liberal dealings, however, with the Ryots, and the exertions of some of my head servants, kept the Ryots to their engagements for some time longer, until three men from Arzool village, Petumber Ghose, Obatah Hazra, and Sreeram Ghose, appeared on the scene. These men were at enmity with me because I had gained an important cause against them in the Civil Court. They had brought a false claim against this concern for some valuable property, which case Mr. Seton Karr dis-missed.   To revenge themselves upon me, or to force me to abandon some of the property they claimed, they took advantage of the insurrection in Kishnaghur, which was inflaming men's minds everywhere, and put themselves at the head of a combination against me.   They made common cause with Harran Joadar, Denoo Kazee, and others (whom I can mention if necessary), collected many hundred of Ryots together, and harangued them on the subject of the indigo disturbances.   I need not mention the particulars of all the arguments they used, but their talk, their persuasions, and their threats, were listened to, and the Ryots were on the point of revolt, when the seizure of two of the ringleaders for the present stopped further mischief.

" The bad seed, however, had been sown, and ·the friends of the three ringleaders were not idle.   Plots were being planned ; and, almost immediately after Pe-tumber and Sreeram Ghose were released from Commer-colly on security, the country became in a blaze.   On the 3rd or 4th instant I was prevented from cutting my indigo in the villages where the Ghoses had influence. My indigo servants were driven from their work, or kept in durance. *My rent cutcherry was looted, my servants staying in the cutcherry were also bound and carried off, and for the present I am completely out of possession of my talook property.*

" As I have fortunately got through my manufacturing without much loss, I should be content to let matters take their course, and allow them to come round in their own good time, for personally I am not now much concerned in what the people in their madness are doing. If they do not sow indigo, I have no wish that they do so ; and as for their not paying me their rents, I am willing to trust to what the law can do for me. But I do not think it consistent with my duties as a member of society, as an English subject, to be silent under circumstances which my Mofussil experience and my local knowledge tell me may lead to great disasters. The disaffection is spreading fast. Many Ryots came to me this morning, saying, that last night agents of Petumber Ghose and Sreeram Ghose had been persuading them and threatening them to join in the conspiracy.

" That I have above represented the true state of affairs I give you my word as a gentleman. I have considered it my duty to do so ; and if you think my communications are worth receiving, I will continue to inform you of what may come under my notice."

Even Mr. Grant will not say, because he cannot say without immediate contradiction, that Mr. Roberts had by tyrannical treatment given any pretence for these kidnappings, and lootings, and combinations. In this letter, which Mr. Grant has published as an official

paper, to shew the planters what he has been able to — —
accomplish for their ruin, Mr. Roberts begs Mr. Harris,
the assistant-magistrate, to inquire and report upon the
truth of the statement he makes.   He says—

" Before informing the higher authorities of certain
facts that have come to my notice, I wish to mention
some of them to you, that you may make inquiries as
to the truth of them, and report upon them should you
think it necessary to do so.   In addition to what I may
state, I will most gladly answer any questions that may
be put to me by you.

" When I took charge of these concerns in October
last, I was most particular in ascertaining personally
from the Ryots whether they had any causes of complaint.   What grievances they had, or pretended to have,
I redressed fully.   I settled their rent complaints to
their satisfaction, paid them higher rates for their ploughs
when they used them for my Neezabad cultivation, increased considerably the price for their indigo plant, for
the cutting, boating, and carting of their indigo, and, in
short, left them no grounds whatever to be dissatisfied
with their business connection with this concern.   They
were well satisfied, and worked cheerfully and readily at
every thing connected with their indigo operations.   I
dwell particularly upon this part of my letter, and beg
your attention to it.   It is a most important point to be
considered, for until the *cause* of the present state of the
country be known and acknowledged, the true remedy
cannot be applied.   That the cause, in this concern, does
not arise from dislike to indigo I have above asserted,
and an important proof of the truth of my assertion is,
that from October to within the last few days no complaint was ever made against me or my servants by any

indigo Ryot.   When it is considered how close my lands are to Magoorah, Commercolly, Khoksa, &c., and that no complaints were made, I hold that this circumstance itself is a *primâ facie* proof that the Ryots had nothing to complain of.   It is well known, that for the last twelve years this concern has had no *power* to force cultivation, and that indigo was sown solely upon the good-will of the Ryots.   The concern had no power to prevent Ryots from complaining, and still with sub-divisions, and stations within hail of my villages, the records of the Courts shew nothing against me.   The enmity now suddenly displayed against this concern is, therefore, altogether without cause."

Such is the state immediately brought about by Mr. J. P. Grant in a peaceful province, after only a few months misgovernment.

CHAPTER VIII.

MR. GRANT THREATENS AND DEPRIVES THE MAGISTRATES.

WE have seen that Mr. Grant had now brought the indigo districts to the verge of a rebellion against all laws of property of every description, and that the Supreme Council had been compelled to interfere by a temporary Act.

This Act provided that Ryots, who had received advances upon their agreements to cultivate indigo during the current season of 1860, should fulfil those agreements : that a Ryot not fulfilling his agreement should forfeit five times the amount advanced and five times the value of the seed ; and that Ryots preventing others by force or intimidation from sowing indigo, or destroying the crop, should be punished by fine and imprisonment.

There was every reason to—what shall we say ? hope or fear ?—that this Act would restore order, and undo all that had been done. The Ryots were returning to the conclusion that the Government were not so much in earnest in the enterprise of driving away the planters ; and that the arrears due to the factories for advances and loans to pay rent and buy bullocks were not to be wiped off. There was a doubt whether Mr. Grant and Mr. Eden, in their cave of Abdullah, would be found a safe refuge for every fraudulent debtor after all. The Ryots began to return to the interrupted negociations for a new arrangement of prices. They said, " If the Government does not wish us not to sow of course we must sow." Grumbling at the Government for deceiving them by a false promise of the division among them of the eight millions of indigo property, they were preparing to sow their indigo lands as usual.

Mr. Grant was for a moment checkmated. The " *gens inimica mihi*" seemed to be safe ; and for a moment he did not see the way to conjure up a new storm. He soon, however, recovered his presence of mind, and he violently restored the former confusion, by abrogating the law and intimidating or removing the magistrates. We cannot dive into Mr. Grant's mind ; we can only judge the motives of men by their acts ; and his acts were those of a man whose projects had been baffled, and whose victims were escaping. Our difficulty is, that the English public will find it almost impossible to believe, that in the present age any head of a department could do what Mr. Grant now did, or that even an Indian officer could dare to interfere with the Act of Council, and with the course of justice. We do not complain that in choosing the magistrates who were to perform the judicial functions under the Act, Mr. Grant chose men of his own way of thinking, so far as he could find them. But having chosen the magistrates, we had a right to expect that he should content himself by sending them out with the Act in their hands to do their duty. Instead of this he sent them forth with a special instruction and a very ominous threat. His instruction is a warning not to put the Act in force. He recounts to them the hardships which they have power to inflict upon the Ryot in that they can now decree " specific performance" of the contract ; and he specially directs them to administer the Act upon " equitable principles." Mr. Grant's own inconceivable ignorance of the rudiments of any civilized judicature appears incontestably from this. He calls the duties of these officials

—which were to punish statutable offence by fine or imprisonment—" the trial of equity suits."*

Imagine a young gentleman of the Civil Service told to administer an Act of Parliament upon equitable principles ! With average intelligence and honesty of intention, which they nearly all shewed themselves to possess, these young men might have seized the plain meaning of a plain Act of legislature; but how were they, or how could Mr. Grant read this Act by the application of those " principles of equity," which still puzzle the sages of Westminster Hall? And what on earth have the " principles of equity" to do with a plain enactment, which says that a man who has had his wages shall do his work, and that if one man prevents his comrade from doing his work he shall be punished for his interference?

Of course Mr. Grant meant by " principles of equity," his own known desires; and lest the magistracy should be slow to comprehend, he added this threat:† " *These* " *powers and the opportunity of acting upon them must not* " *be retained for a day in the hands of any officer who may* " *shew himself not competent to exercise them in such a man-* " *ner as to do full and ample justice to all parties.*" Every magistrate could guess what this meant, and no one was in ignorance of what Mr. Grant meant when he talked of

* See par. 23 of Mr. Grant's Minute, in answer to the Planters' Petition against him.

† The planters, in their Petition, allude to this as a threat, and Mr. Grant, in his reply, says—" This is a misrepresentation." It is not usual in political controversy thus curtly to give the lie. Since the Civil Service are, according to the Report of the House of Commons Colonization Committee, " the nobility of India," we might suggest to Mr. Grant that—*noblesse oblige.* There is nothing for it but to return the contradiction and submit the proof. We have now quoted the passage of his letter, and we shall shew how severely the " THREAT" was fulfilled. We ask the English public to judge who has been guilty of " misrepresentation,"—this rather unmannerly minister or his remonstrating victims.

" *substantial justice,*" as distinguished from legal justice, between a Ryot and a planter.

But lest there should still be any chance of this Act being allowed to be put in force, Mr. Grant, finding that the Act allowed no appeal in these cases, supplied one of his own authority. He says, in par. 6 of his circular letter—" As the legislature allows no appeal from the decisions of officers vested with powers under this Act, it becomes doubly incumbent *on commissioners to keep themselves constantly informed* of the manner in which these officers discharge the very difficult responsible duty now imposed upon them, *and of the principles by which they are guided in their decisions.*"

This was tolerably strong. It was a violent and illegal subordination of the judicial officers of the country to the revenue officer of the district. But even this would not do. Most of the officers read the Act in its natural sense, and put it in force against ringleaders and intimidators. Mr. Grant now had to go a step further. He came out with a new law of evidence. Mr. Herschel, one of the officers, had, he found, been admitting the planters' books and the oath of a native servant of the factory as evidence of receipt of the advances. Probably Mr. Herschel had somehow become acquainted with the fact that this is the every-day proof of a debt in the English Courts. Mr. Grant, in a letter from the Secretary of Government to the Commissioner of Nuddea, reprimands him roundly, and Mr. Herschel is so amenable to this advice, that he soon afterwards gives a decision entirely in accordance with all Mr. Grant's views. Mr. Grant is so pleased with it, that he has it printed and sent round the district for imitation. It was against all law and against all justice. Introduced into England, it would upset society. It was founded upon the

wholesale rejection or disbelief of the books and documents kept according to the common practice of all indigo
factories, and, indeed, of all traders of every class.

The Lieutenant-Governor now proceeded to fulfil his
threat not to trust the administration of this Act for a day
in the hands of any man who did not decide according to,
not to what is law, but to what is, according to Mr.
Grant's views, substantial justice between a Ryot and a
planter. He promoted Mr. Herschel over the heads of
his seniors; he removed men who opened their ears to
evidence on the planters' side; he confirmed every one
who with a tolerably certain consistency decided one way,
and against a planter ; and he moved all the oldest civilians out of the country.

Having thus ordered their six months Indigo Contracts' Act to be read by the light of the principles of
equity—whether as derived from the Institutes of Justi-
nian, or from the Equity Text-books, Mr. Grant does not
say—and having dismissed or removed those officers who
did not answer the whip; having, further, made a great
alteration in the law of evidence, by discountenancing the
only evidence of his credits which the planter could be
expected to possess ; Mr. Grant now took occasion to give
a signal triumph to the Ryots, who had been seduced by
his proclamations; for, reversing the judgments of the
magistrates, he let the convicted offenders off their fines
and out of prison.

Now, to a certain extent this was unjustly honourable.
Having incited these people to break their contracts, it
was a matter of personal honour with Mr. Grant, so long
as he was allowed to retain power, to abuse it to protect
these people from the consequences of acting upon his
advice, and that of his co-operating underlings. But he
carried this too far: there was no need to extend this

entire impunity to cases where the offence was intimidating other Ryots who wished to sow, or ploughing up land which they had sown.

Mr. Grant had now contrived to extract from this Act, intended by the Supreme Council for the preservation of the planters, means to accelerate their ruin. The Council had granted special powers of enforcing the contracts of one season. Mr. Grant had contrived, by tampering with the course of justice, to render it nearly impotent for that purpose, and had also contrived to give the natives the notion that this Act abrogated all agreements so far as they extended beyond the current year. What was intended as a boon, became, in Mr. Grant's hands, a scourge. What was intended to neutralize the effect of Mr. Eden's perwannahs, became, under Mr. Grant's explanations, an absolute ratification of them, so far as all the contracts for three years are concerned. "It must be stated," says Mr. Grant, "that it is the desire of the Government that those Ryots who have received cash advances* upon their agreement to cultivate indigo *during the current season* shall honestly fulfil that agreement." A tolerably obvious suggestion to the Bengali mind that it was the desire of the Government that the Ryot should not "honestly fulfil his agreement" beyond the current season; although for this suggestion Mr. Grant had no more authority from the Supreme Council than he would have had to desire one of

---

* The Act was one for the summary fulfilment of contracts. The insertion of the words "cash advances" was most unjustifiable and injurious. It was meant, and the Act was worked according to such meaning, that unless a Ryot had actually touched "cash" during the current season, he was not liable under the law. A Ryot, and this is a very common case, may have received five times the amount of his usual advance the previous year by way of loan for a marriage, or for purchase of cattle, the sum being carried to account, to be liquidated in three or four years. Not having taken "cash" this year, he was free of his contract!

Ameer Mullick's gang of dacoits to steal Mr. Larmour's watch.*

The planters now saw ruin staring them in the face. The Englishman who had been placed in supreme power over Bengal, to protect all classes, had outlawed his countrymen, and had excited the natives against them. The planters saw that it was in vain to expostulate with this man. His tender mercies were cruelties. Never, at their prayer, did he profess to move in their favour, or to put out a proclamation with the pretended object of calming excitement, but by some strange fatality it was found to have a directly opposite effect. The planters now presented a petition against Mr. Grant.

The petitioners in that sober and measured language, which contrasts conspicuously with the vague accusations, and the contemptuous contradictions of Mr. Grant, state the circumstances out of which these unhappy dissensions arose; call attention to the admitted ignorance of Mr. Grant upon the subject of indigo culture;† complain of the acts of Mr. Eden; but especially appeal against the despotic acts—nay, worse than despotic acts, for even a despot has generally an instinct in favour of the purity of justice, when he himself is not a party—by which Mr.

* The planters, in their petition against Mr. Grant, make it one of their complaints, " that in several districts contracts have been entered into for three years and upwards, and in the absence of any legislative enactment to the contrary, such contracts are in every way binding, and many planters have made their calculations for the several seasons on the knowledge of these contracts; but His Honour, without taking this fact into consideration, or indeed considering for one instant the serious effect on all cultivators of indigo of such a proceeding, lately published a proclamation, the immediate effect of which was to cause the Ryots in many districts, who were previously perfectly quiet, and especially in Messrs. Watson and Co.'s factories, to combine against their employers."

† Mr. Grant having once fairly admitted " that he had never had any experience in the indigo districts, and that he was very ignorant on the subject," has since desired to recall this inconvenient, although most true admission.

Grant turned aside the operation of the "Indigo Contracts Act."

Perhaps it will be better that the reader should have before him the language of the petition in this important matter. It complains—

" That, considering the powers which His Honour has, as to the removal of magistrates, it was, as your Petitioners submit, uncalled for—unless the Honourable Lieutenant-Governor could not trust the magisterial officers of the district—to hold out, as he did in the letter No. 1, a threat of removal if any magistrate interpreted the Act contrary to His Honour's views.

"That the Lieutenant-Governor, in laying down rules for the interpretation of the Act, exceeded, as your Petitioners submit, his powers, and trespassed upon the province of the Legislative Council, and of the Judicial Officers of the Government, because, where a question as to the meaning of an Act arose; a judicial tribunal, where both sides could be heard, was the proper forum to interpret it.

"That your Petitioners beg to draw to the earnest consideration of your Excellency in Council, that the Lieutenant-Governor has, since that Act was passed, interfered with the working of it in such a way as to make it wholly useless for the purpose which the Legislative Council had in view; and your Petitioners have only to refer to the records of the Government of Bengal containing the papers relative to indigo planting, which are published by authority, to shew that His Honour had exercised an improper and most indiscreet interference with sentences passed by the magistrates.

"That soon after the passing of the Act, a Mooktear was tried by Mr. Betts for instigating Ryots to break their engagements, and a number of Ryots were sentenced for ploughing up indigo that had been sown.

"That both of these offences had become very common, and it was necessary, for the sake of example, to put them down at once; but notwithstanding this, and the express provision by the Legislative Council that there should be no appeal, the Lieutenant-Governor, on the 19th April, 1860, ordered the Commissioner to review these proceedings, as appears by the letter hereto annexed, and marked No. 3.

" *That by adopting such a course, the prosecutors had not even the chance, which, if there had been an appeal, they would have had, of shewing that the convictions were proper ;* and the Lieutenant-Governor soon afterwards ordered the release of the Mooktear and the Ryots, which did more harm than your Excellency can imagine.

" That, in order to shew what the wish of His Honour was, this proceeding has been followed up by his directing the release of many other Ryots imprisoned duly according to law, and *the removal from the indigo districts of the magistrates, Messrs. Betts, Mackenzie, M'Niell, and Taylor,* and the substitution for them, in cases coming under the new Act, of some of the Principal Sudder Ameens of other districts.

"That the effect of His Honour's interference has, amongst other things, been to create an impression, not only in the *minds of the magistrates, but also of the planters and Ryots, that any decisions in favour of the planters would meet with the disapproval of the Government of Bengal;* and your Petitioners would beg leave to draw the attention of your Excellency in Council to the evidence, amongst others, of Mr. Furlong and Mr. Taylor, given before the Indigo Commissioners (the evidence on oath of men of the most unimpeachable character), to shew the effect of these acts of His Honour, and the absurdity of continuing to institute suits under the new Act.

"That in a recent case, in which a decision has been given by Mr. Herschel, magistrate of Kishnaghur, which your Petitioners consider to be entirely contrary to the evidence, and most unjust to the planter concerned, His Honour has, upon a special report of the case to him, ordered copies of it to be distributed among the officials before whom cases under Act XI. of 1860 are tried, with an intimation that Mr. Herschel's decision is to be taken as a rule to guide them in all similar cases. This your Petitioners look upon as a most unusual and unauthorized interference with the ordinary course of law, and the proper independence of the judicial authorities, and especially unfair and injurious to your Petitioners, inasmuch as the evidence produced was chiefly that of books and documents, kept according to the common practice of all indigo factories, which are thereby, and in this particular case, unjustly condemned wholesale, as not to be received as good evidence of claims against Ryots; and, being the only corroborative evidence planters have to produce, such claims are practically rendered impossible of proof.

"That your Petitioners beg to draw particular attention to the evidence of Mr. Taylor, a man of the highest honour and reputation, given before the Commissioners, by which it appears, that while the decision of cases under Act XI. was left to the gentlemen acting as magistrates in the district, every case was decided in his favour, every case which has, since their removal, been brought by him before the Principal Sudder Ameen, although supported by the same class of evidence as in the previous cases, has been dismissed; a fact that, as your Petitioners submit, shews the effect of the interference which they now complain of."

After making these very precise charges the planters prayed very modestly—

"Your Petitioners, therefore, humbly pray, your Excellency in Council to take into consideration this Petition, and to pass such orders as may oblige His Honour the Lieutenant-Governor of Bengal to refrain from pursuing a course of conduct which cannot but be ruinous to the indigo planters in Bengal, and to point out to His Honour the impropriety of interfering with

" the due course of the administration of the law by the
" regularly appointed judicial officers, as laid down by
" the Legislative Council of India, and which interference
" is, as your Petitioners submit, both illegal and uncon-
" stitutional, and especially indiscreet in the case of a
" dispute between capital and labour ; and that your Ex-
" cellency may pass such further orders as may, under
" the above circumstances, seem proper."

Such are the accusations not only made, but substan-
tiated against this high officer. To bring them home to
an English mind we must imagine that any Home Secretary for the time being, had first wantonly interfered in
a question of prices between some classes of employers
and employed ; that he had excited the labourers to leave
their jobs unperformed ; that when the Parliament had
passed a new law to meet the juncture, the Home Secretary had chosen special magistrates to work the law, had
threatened them with dismissal if they did not interpret
it according to his notorious partiality ; that he had circulated a form of decision among them ; that he had promoted those who obeyed his commands as to how they
should decide ; and that he had suspended and removed
others who had conscientiously disobeyed him. This is
what Mr. Grant has done in Bengal. Thus far he admits the facts. He does not dispute them. All he does
is vindictively to abuse the men whom he dismissed.

However, this petition drew from Mr. Grant a Minute
of seventeen folio pages.

The reader who has any recollection of the letters which
we have copied from Mr. Grant's own government papers,
and which have described the repudiation of contracts,
the looting of factories, and the refusal of rents, may be
able to measure the robustness of Mr. Grant's confidence
in the credulity of the English public when he finds that

Mr. Grant's reply to the charge, that he has thrown the indigo districts into confusion, is a bold assertion that "those districts are not in confusion." He adds—"the indigo districts, and Kishnaghur especially, in every general sense are perfectly tranquil." The "particular" sense, we presume, is the planters' sense. Or is it *solitudinem facit, pacem appellat?* Is it the tranquillity of which Mr. Roberts has spoken? To such audacity as this the decencies of language offer no form of reply. All it is possible to say is, that it is publicly and notoriously not true. "A timely display of force," he says, "saved the indigo factories." It seems, then, according to his own shewing, to be the "tranquillity" which depends upon the presence of an armed force "saving" the Europeans from murder and pillage. So far from seeing any thing to regret in this, it is just what Mr. Grant intimates satisfies all his wishes. There may be a necessity for "a timely display of force;" but let the planters be reassured. Mr. Grant tells them with a pleasant sarcasm, the burnished point of which they can admire while they are listening for the shouts of the insurgent Ryots, that, "practically the life, property, rights, and personal liberty, even of the humblest cultivator, were never before more secure than they now are in those districts." We do not know whether the fact detracts at all from the cleverness of this serio-comic assurance, but it is remarkable that precisely the same words might have been addressed by Nana Sahib, and with perfect truth, to the victims at Cawnpore.

The reader will see, that when these poor planters come to the Government with ruined prospects, with their indigo plantations trampled out, with their credits—which Mr. Grant says are, with their vats, all their capital —

confiscated, some with their factories "looted," and all with their lives in jeopardy, they find Mr. Grant in a fine taunting mood, and in most exuberant spirits. He congratulates them that "since the abduction of Seetal Turufdar — whose death under circumstances which appear to make the whole affair amount to murder—he had not heard of a single case of lawless violence in Nuddea." Of course he did not mean to say that he intended to take trials for murder out of the regular judges' hands, and to find upon the spot that Seetal Turufdar (of whom no planter knew any more than he did of the abduction of young Mortara and the murder of the child at Road) was abducted, and was wifully murdered, and that he then and there found all the planters guilty of the crime. He did not mean this, but he wanted to say something smart, and to throw a stone at those insolent planters who had presumed to bring their plebeian charges against his high mightiness. If he had not been a civilian and his accusers had been, he would probably have referred to some notorious case of dirty venality in some dead-and-gone member of the Civil service ; but as it is, he mentions the name of a murdered native, and suggests that, as they were planters, of course they must know something about it; just as, when a little Christian boy was missed about passover time, all the Christians used to insist that the Jews knew all about it, and had undoubtedly taken him away to sacrifice him.

After this specimen of what we cannot refrain from calling ill breeding, Mr. Grant slips naturally into a string of unmitigated—what shall we call them ?—they are not truths—for thousands of respectable men on their oaths will disprove every proposition as it comes out. We must fall back upon Mr. Grant's admitted ignorance, and call them —mistakes. He says—"Even in matters relating to the present commercial disagreement, law and justice prevail." We have shewn pretty conclusively how conspicuously untrue this is. Again, " The persons and property of planters are everywhere inviolate." What! are a man's credits no part of his property? Are the reports of the Civil servants who describe the withholding of rents not worthy of belief, even when Mr. Grant himself publishes them? Has he not himself told us that the factories were only saved by a timely display of force? But see how trenchantly Mr. Grant wades through the standing facts. He does not hesitate to say, " Whilst on the one hand planters do not carry off, by unlawful force, indigo plant in the lawful possession of other people; on the other hand, if they advanced a single copper pice for any indigo plant, to which they have a claim under a contract, but of which they have a difficulty in obtaining delivery, they have now the means of establishing the fact, and obtaining possession legally, in three or four days." After what we have shewn, the curious reader must smile as he recognises this careful string of prevarications. No one knows better than Mr. Grant that this phrase " lawful possession of other people" means only a robbery under Mr. Grant's protection. True, the planter cannot get possession of the indigo which he has bought, because Mr. Grant will not allow the magistrates to do justice, and carry out the law. Mr. Grant insults the planter by shewing him his indigo in his debtors' hands; and tantalizes him by telling him that this is become " lawful possession." The next, however, is still stronger :—" Where no contracts and advances are established, we have reports of planters and their European assistants going about themselves amongst the Ryots, and actually paying for the plant, to the owner's content, in cash on the field." Now we ask Mr. Grant upon his honour — not whether he has such reports, for he may, as we well know, have any reports he pleases to order, but — will he say that he believes there is in all Bengal a piece of indigo ready for cutting upon which no advances have been paid to the Ryot? He does not believe it. He knows that such a thing is unheard of and impossible. If it be a fact that planters have been this season buying ready-grown indigo, the only possible inference is this — that under Mr. Grant's protection, the Ryot is selling to strangers the indigo which he has raised at the cost of the planter; while those to whom it morally, and even legally belongs, look on without remedy.

This is not a defence. It is a triumphant avowal of the oppression he has been practising, and the ruin he has been inflicting. It is a song of triumph, a war-whoop over his victims. It seems to say, " What have you got from the Supreme Council?" " Make the most of your Act." " Establish your advances if you can." There is a taunting sneer in this answer which may pass undetected by our home Ministers and our home public, but which is well understood in India. Possibly, during those six months in which the " Indigo Contracts Act" was in force, any planter who could " establish" an advance might obtain his indigo. But it must have been established in face of the power of Mr. Grant. Well may Mr. Grant chuckle over the difficulty of such an achievement. Small chance was there of a planter " establishing" his title to 13,000 plots of indigo against the opposition of a Lieutenant-Governor, who interfered with the course of justice, ordered the judges to disregard the evidence of the planters' books, removed some judges when they decided in favour of the planters, and so thoroughly frightened the others, that at last every judge felt that it was equivalent to dismissal, to allow himself to be convinced by any evidence that a planter had made an advance. Small hope was there in continuing to manufacture indigo in face of an absolute Governor, who let Ryots convicted of making depredations upon a planter, out of prison, but fiercely pounced upon every planter's servant who attempted to defend his master's property. Small chance was there of prevailing against a Governor whose examples were pardons for crimes against morality and order, and severe punishments for every act which was a moral right, but a legal wrong. Mr. Grant may well tauntingly congratulate the planters with the doubtful advantage of the Summary Act while he was by ; but it required a degree of hatred, which, in its triumph had cast away all prudence, to glory in the fact that by means of his interference with the course of justice, the Ryot was enabled to carry away his plunder under the eye of the planter, and to sell it in public market.

This is the whole gist of Mr. Grant's answer to specific charges. He does not attempt to deny that he dismissed the magistrates, or issued the pattern decision, or reversed the sentences, or set the Commissioners to overlook the magistrates. He assumes that the elder and more experienced magistrates, whom he recalled or suspended, were deciding erroneously, and that the decision of Mr. Herschel, a very young officer,* who, after a strong hint from

* These youthful appointments have their advantages and their disadvantages. Under a fair Governor they work well ; but under a tyrannical and unjust Governor, youth more easily takes the mould of the superior.

Mr. Grant, disbelieved the planters' books, was a model decision, and deserved to be circulated for imitation. He denies, with an effrontery which makes us wonder whether Mr. Grant applies his notions of "equitable principles" of interpretation, to morals as well as to law, that he "ever so much as expressed an opinion regarding the interpretation of the Act," or he "ever in any single instance interpreted the Act."* He justifies the removal

Mr. MacNair, in his evidence before the Colonization Committee, 1858, seems to be influenced by what he had recently seen.

"2000. *Chairman.*] Will you proceed with your statement?—The exclusive system of the Civil Service is also very objectionable. Of late years so many of the more experienced and able gentlemen of that service have been taken away for new and advanced employment, and been absent from the country, that a great many mere youths, a few months from college, with little knowledge of the language, and with no experience or business habits, are placed in charge of large districts. It cannot be expected that they could have any control over their court servants or over the police, consequently the business is entirely in the hands of the native omlah, who soon know their power, and use it for their own advantage. I have known court omlahs with the small salary of ten to twelve rupees per month, accumulating large sums in a few years, and purchasing landed property, and building pukka houses. There are no doubt many very able men in the service, who take an interest in their work, and give general satisfaction. The most able men are generally made collectors, as I suppose Government think it most important to collect the revenues. The inexperienced youths are made magistrates ; and the higher judicial appointments are filled by people whose energies are expended, and who are anxious to take the earliest opportunity of retiring from the service, which they can do upon a handsome pension, after an actual service of twenty-two years. If these appointments were open to competition in India, many well-qualified people would be found able to fill them ; and it would also be a great inducement for English settlers to qualify themselves for those appointments where they would get advancement from their own merits and exertions. At present the uncovenanted deputy-magistrates and deputy-collectors of experience and long-standing get about the same allowance as the young civilians get when they receive their appointments. I think it would be very advantageous to put the covenanted and uncovenanted services upon the same footing as it is in this country, and open the Civil Service entirely."—*Evidence of Mr. G. MacNair, Colonization Committee,* 1858.

* Mr. Grant should have a longer memory. In par. 7 of his Circular he says, " But it must also be explained that *the order extends only to*

of Mr. Betts, because he had, in favour of a planter, given effect to a contract which bore a date earlier than that on which the stamp was sold. In the vivid imagination of Mr. Grant, a mere clerical error becomes a grave charge of forgery against a planter ; in the mind of Mr. Grant the fault of not sharing this extravagant error is a sufficient cause for removing a judge.*   Mr. Grant admits (par. 36), that

---

the current season ; and it is the intention of Government, before the period of taking advances for next season arrives to," &c. &c. Now this is not only an interpretation, but it is a very false and a very fatal interpretation. It induced the Ryots erroneously to believe that the Act annulled all contracts beyond the current season ; and it is an interpretation which is at this moment paralyzing the trade of the indigo manufacturer.

* The planters were naturally very much incensed at a charge of forgery publicly brought by a Lieut.-Governor, without even a shadow of reason, and in order to defend his own misconduct, against one of their body. The story of this caluminous assertion is so extraordinary that we refrain from stating it ourselves, and prefer to quote the account of it given by the Times' Calcutta Correspondent, in the Times of the 22nd November, 1860 : —

" Calcutta, Oct. 18th.

" I enclose herewith the reply given by the Indigo Planters' Association to the charges brought against the entire body of planters by Mr. Grant, to which I have before referred. I cannot send at the same time the documents alluded to in this reply, because they have all been sent up to the Governor-General. I am able, nevertheless, to assure you that they fully and entirely bear out every allegation contained in this document. The two points which, in his famous Minute, he urged most strongly against the planters were,—first, their enlisting the younger magistrates on their behalf, and so acting upon them as to induce them to give decisions in their favour, and even in one instance to sentence the legal adviser of the ryots to imprisonment merely for doing his duty towards his clients ; secondly, their obtaining decrees by means of forged agreements, illustrating his argument by citing a case in which a decree was given on a written agreement purporting to have been made in 1856, though executed on stamped paper which, on investigation, was proved to have been sold in 1859. On these two charges, which Mr. Grant treated as cases fully proved, requiring no further examination, he rang the changes until, to his own satisfaction, he proved the planters guilty of every description of oppression. It now appears that both these charges were utterly false. This is no mere assertion on my part ; it is proved by the strongest evidence ; in the first case, by the records of the Court in which the case was tried ;

H

before his interference the Civil Magistrates usually found that the planters adduced sufficient proof of their having made advances, whereas since that time "the same sort of claims have been, for the most part, rejected upon the question of fact;" and he thus grants the truth of the planters' complaint, that under the carefully packed staff of magistrates which Mr. Grant at last placed in office, "the absurdity of continuing to institute suits under the new Act," becomes altogether manifest.

Surely this is enough. We should be quite satisfied to rest the case upon the admissions contained in Mr. Grant's apology. Of course it is open to any one who interferes with the course of justice to allege that he did so from a good motive. All the creatures of the Stuart kings could say as much. Mr. Grant really seems incapable of understanding that it is a crime to defeat the free course of justice. He seems to think, that if he can induce people to believe that his motives were good, the charge of tampering with the administration of the law is answered. He has not even got so far into the rudiments of natural justice as to know, that the Governor

in the second, by the agreement itself, which is a true *bond fide* document, and which has been sent up to the Governor-General for his inspection. The letter was only submitted to-day to the Government and therefore I can give you no idea as to the reception it will meet with. This, however, is certain—that people out of doors entertain a strong hope that Lord Canning's eyes will be opened to the real merits of the " system " which has been put in practice against the planters. I may add, with reference to this case, that it was with the greatest difficulty that the planters could obtain sight of the document which Mr. Grant asserted to have been forged, but which has since proved to be genuine. For nearly three weeks the secretary of the Planters' Association exerted himself to procure it, and it was only when the authorities were driven either to give it or refuse it absolutely, that the request was complied with. The cases I have referred to present by no means exaggerated instances of the system which has been employed during the current year to drive the planter out of the country."

who tampers with the judgment-seat becomes at once the greatest criminal in the court he violates. What Lieut.-Governor Grant's object was, we cannot conclude, except from the results he has obtained. He has gone nigh *to destroy* one of the most important industries which it was his sworn duty to protect.

Still less is it necessary to follow Mr. Grant into topics extraneous to the deliberate charge we have made against him, or to rectify his mis-statements when he has recourse to the stale and threadbare device of varying this charge, while he pretends to repeat it.* Nor need we discuss with Mr. Grant those two "opinions amongst

---

* We charge him with publishing to the Ryots a false and most mischievous account of the Summary Act of 1860, and he thus mis-states the charge :—

"If it is meant that the Executive Government, whilst leaving to the Legislature the outward show and pretence of fair intention, should have quietly allowed the law to be understood in the Mofussil, and acted upon, as though it had been a law to force Ryots, being Her Majesty's free subjects, to cultivate indigo, whether they wished to do so or not, at prices fixed by the purchaser, though they might be under no obligation to do so, and though they might never have received a farthing of consideration—such an Act, in short, as no Legislature would have dared to put into plain words—His Excellency in Council will not expect me to notice the complaint."—*Minute,* par. 19.

Again.—We accuse him of interfering with the course of justice, threatening and removing officers of justice who do not carry out his partial views, and circulating pattern decisions, which are contrary both to law and to natural justice. The innocent man replies in this fashion :—

"I have always thought, and I continue to think, the law will be self-acting and complete in the natural course of things, under a legitimate, vigorous, and truly impartial magisterial action ; which, leaving disputes in Civil cases to be settled by the constituted Civil tribunals, abstaining from all support of either party not warranted by the law, and, founding itself wholly on the law, will give that equal protection from unlawful violence to both parties, in practice, which the law, in theory, has always intended. I accept all responsibilities for holding this opinion, and for acting upon it, so far as the occasion required, whenever the necessity of so doing has been forced by circumstances upon me."—*Minute,* par. 15 and 16. Alas! as Madame Parnelle says of Tartufe—"La vertu dans le monde est toujours poursuivie."

disinterested persons, whether any special law against
the Ryots was justifiable under the circumstances or
not." His duty was, not to balance opinions whether
the law was "justifiable," but to obey it, just as it was;
not to send out judges to decide as he might wish, but to
send out judges to decide. We decline to enter upon
any such extraneous topics. If we go beyond facts capable of proof, we get into floods of feeble rhetoric, point-
less sarcasm, and spiteful retorts, which seem to aim at
bitterness, but achieve only an unmannerly incivility.
We have no taste for a contest of this kind. What we
very deeply feel, however, while reading this apology, is,
that Mr. Grant does not seem to be capable of that impartial habit of mind which would enable him to comprehend that even planters may have rights; and what we
are sometimes compelled to doubt is, whether upon this
subject Mr. Grant, when under the influence of his prejudices, has sufficient clearness of intellect even to understand the tendency of an argument.*

---

* Thus, when we had proved that Mr. Grant suspended or removed
the officers who shewed an inclination to hold the scales even, and that he
had refused to remove a gentleman who was ignoring all the "paper
evidence" of the planters, Mr. Grant answers us with the following in-
coherent absurdity:—

"It will not be contended that unqualified officers should be removed
when the complaint comes from one side, but should not be removed
when it comes from the other side. Yet unless this principle be contended for, the complaint by the Association of the removal of Mr. Betts
is as little to be justified as their complaint of the removal of the three
other gentlemen named, who have not been removed."—*Minute*, par. 33.

CHAPTER IX.

THE INDIGO COMMISSION OF 1860, AND ITS TWIN REPORT.

WHILE the indigo districts had been thus coaxed into a state of general repudiation of their debts and contracts; while the Summary Act of the Supreme Council was being thus detorted by the Lieut.-Governor of Bengal; and while the Ryots were complaining of the treachery of Government in first exciting them to repudiate, and then passing an Act to compel them to perform, Mr. Grant attempted to keep up the courage of the Ryots and calm the outcries of the planters, by promising a commission of inquiry which should set all things to rights.

He kept his promise in this wise :—

He constituted a commission of five members—two civilians, a Missionary, a native employed in an inferior office under Government, and a merchant.

The composition of this body shews at once what Mr. Grant's intention was in creating it. There could be no reason why the Missionary body should have a seat at this board, except that one or two German missionaries have, unhappily, upon several occasions, lent their aid to give currency to the thrice-refuted calumnies invented against the planters.* There could be no good reason

---

* There is a very false notion abroad that the Missionary body have testified against the planters. Nothing can be more unfounded. The testimony of all the English Missionaries is uniformly in consonance

why a native of high standing and intelligence should not be chosen, except that he might happen to share the sen-

with that of the Governors General, magistrates and natives we have already cited. Some *German* Missionaries have indeed upon one occasion committed themselves to some monstrous statements, but those who know India will understand what they mean. We will subjoin a few extracts from the statements of the Missionary body upon this subject.

Let us take first the evidence of Mr. Underhill, the Secretary of the Baptist Missionary Society, who had been on special mission in India. In his examination before the Colonization Committee, 1859, this gentleman states :—

"4778. *Mr. Kinnaird.*] What bearing might the increase of European landholders have upon the welfare of the Ryots ?—On the whole, I have no doubt that it would be highly beneficial; it appears to me that the tendency of all European occupation is to improve both the productions of the land and the condition of those who labour upon the land; one might be sure that this is the case, from the general contentment of the servants of the different English Zemindars."

And again :—

"4771. *Mr. Kinnaird.*] Has there not been much controversy between the indigo planters and the Missionaries, arising out of these circumstances ?—There was a great deal just previously to my leaving for England, arising from the statement of a German Missionary in Kishnaghur, that the indigo planting system was a system of great oppression and extortion on the Ryot; but the conclusion to which I came, after a great deal of thought and conversation with parties interested in the matter, was what I have already stated, that almost universally those oppressions and extortions originate in the state of the country, in the state of the administration of the law, in the character of the police, and in difficulties which the indigo planter might well plead in bar of any condemnation that might be brought upon conduct that otherwise we must very strongly condemn."

Once more, this gentleman, who may be taken to represent the whole Baptist body upon this matter, says :—

"4709. Will you generally state the results of your observation on the residence of Europeans in the country ?—There can be no doubt whatever that the residence of Europeans in the interior is highly beneficial in a material sense by the introduction of new products and new modes of producing articles of commerce ; a great improvement is already seen in the rise of wages through almost the whole of those parts of Bengal where Europeans reside. Then you may see the influence of Europeans always when you come within a few miles of the places where they dwell ; the country is better cultivated, the roads are in better order, and the aspect of the land itself bears the impress of European skill and European capital having been expended upon it, so

timents of such men as Dwarkanauth Tagore and Rammohun Roy.*   That there should be one merchant was a

that you can very readily tell whether you are approaching any settlement, or factory, or farm inhabited by Europeans.   Then, in a social sense, I think also the presence of Europeans is highly beneficial.   In former days many Europeans lived very improper lives in India: that day is gone by; I am very glad to say that that has almost entirely ceased, and that the Europeans now living in the Mofussil are not addicted to the immoral habits which were very common 30, 40, or 50 years ago.   Then, I think also that the influence of Europeans is exceedingly beneficial, from the diffusion of the ideas of truth and justice which they invariably maintain; whatever a European may be in other respects, his word is always taken by natives, and, with very rare exceptions, they always confide in a European's judgment, and upon his general equity they constantly rely; they seem to think that a European will always do them justice if he can, if his own special and peculiar interests do not clash with what the native may seem to think just."

We would refer also to the letter from Dr. Duff, that eminent Presbyterian divine, which has been printed in the Appendix to the Indigo Report, 1860.

Mr. Marshman stated to the Colonization Committee:—

"9586. I have known, as I have mentioned to the Committee, indigo planters who were regarded as the fathers of the Ryots around them; men like Mr. Furlong, and half a dozen other gentlemen I could name, who spared no expense and no labour in order to benefit the Ryots around them."

It would be easy to multiply proof of what we have advanced, and it would also be easy to adduce passages wherein Missionaries have deplored the bad state of the law which leads to occasional disputes, and sometimes to violent quarrels; but upon the whole, the English Missionaries are very truthful and impartial in their account of the indigo manufacturer, not of course as perfect creatures, but as upon the whole a great blessing to India.   With the Germans we desire to have no connection, either amicable or hostile, and we must be allowed to pass their absurd misstatements without notice.

* In page 176 of the papers relating to the conduct of Europeans in India, the opinions of these two eminent natives are thus recorded:—

"Dwarkanauth Tagore said—'With reference to the subject more immediately before the meeting, I beg to state that I have several Zemindaries in various districts, and that I have found that the cultivation of indigo, and the residence of Europeans, have considerably benefited the community at large; the Zemindars becoming wealthy and prosperous; the Ryots *materially improved in their condition, and possessing many more comforts than the generality of my countrymen where indigo cultivation and manufacture are not carried on;* the value

matter of course.   Perhaps we are not unreasonable in thinking that there might have been also one practical indigo planter.   We do not dispute either the propriety of having two civilians on the commission, nor could a more intelligent or upright civilian have been found than Mr. Temple, who was Secretary to Mr. Wilson, and was chosen and trusted by that shrewd and careful minister, as the most liberal and widely-informed member of that body.

We cannot, however, pass over the appointment of Mr.

of land in the vicinity to be considerably enhanced, and cultivation rapidly progressing.   I do not make these statements merely from hearsay, *but from personal observation and experience, as I have visited the places referred to repeatedly,* and, in consequence, am well acquainted with the character and manners of the indigo planters.   There may be a few exceptions, as regards the general conduct of indigo planters, but they are extremely limited, and, comparatively speaking, of the most trifling importance.   I may be permitted to mention an instance in support of this statement.   Some years ago, when indigo was not so generally manufactured, one of my estates, where there was no cultivation of indigo, did not yield a sufficient income to pay the Government assessment : but within a few years, by the introduction of indigo, there is now not a beegah on the estate untilled, and it gives me a handsome profit.   Several of my relations and friends, whose affairs I am well acquainted with, have in like manner improved their property, and are receiving a large income from their estates."

"Rammohun Roy used the following language :—' From personal experience I am impressed with the conviction, that the greater our intercourse with European gentlemen, the greater will be our improvement in literary, social, and political affairs ; a fact which can be easily proved, by comparing the condition of those of my countrymen who have enjoyed this advantage, with that of those who unfortunately have not that opportunity ; and a fact which I could, to the best of my belief, declare on solemn oath before any assembly.   I fully agree with Dwarkanauth Tagore in the purport of the resolution just read.   As to the indigo planters, I beg to observe, *that I have travelled through several districts in Bengal and Behar, and I found the natives residing in the neighbourhood of indigo plantations evidently better clothed and better conditioned than those who lived at a distance from such stations.* There may be some partial injury done by the indigo planters; but on the whole, *they have performed more good to the generality of the natives of this country than any other class of Europeans, whether in or out of the* SERVICE."

Seton Karr. This gentleman was known to be a partisan. From the year 1847, when he wrote a rather clever article upon indigo in the *Calcutta Review*, he had gradually risen under the patronage of Mr. Grant, and had strengthened into a famous planter-hater. He was now, of course, a satellite of Mr. Grant. Further than this, while he was yet sitting as President of the Commission, and while the Report was yet undrawn, Mr. Seton Karr was appointed Secretary to Mr. Grant. As President of the Commission his animus appears in every examination; he drew the Report, which incorrectly assumes the character of the Report of the Commission; and, even after it was signed, he made several offensive additions to it.

We submit that this appointment of Mr. Seton Karr, under these circumstances, and at this crisis, was a violation even of the decencies of official hypocrisy. It was no more in fact than Mr. Grant had done before in working, or rather in destroying, the Summary Act. But still it was a contempt of appearances. Mr. Grant is not in a position to ask us to assume, as a matter of course, that he and his Secretary are heroes of superhuman virtue, and that the ordinary objects of official life can be dangled before their eyes without any effect.

The result was very much what might have been anticipated: Mr. Seton Karr, the Missionary,* and the

---

* Of course Mr. Seton Karr's Report is a series of compromises. Mr. Sale, we will hope, insisted upon one line, out of the forty-eight folio pages, in mention of the opium cultivation as having features identical with the indigo cultivation; he also obtained a paragraph absolving the Missionaries in which, as we have already stated, we heartily concur, so far as the English as contradistinguished from the German Missionaries are intended. But we should very much like to have some competent investigation into the conduct of the foreigners. In Mr. Furlong's evidence before the Commission, the following passage occurs: "Mr. Bomwetsch, of Santiporc, has openly preached a crusade against indigo

Baboo, agreed to a report; Mr. Temple signed the report
with a protest against all the really important parts of
it;* Mr. Ferguson protested against the whole report;†
and Mr. Temple and Mr. Fergusson joined in a report of
fifty-three paragraphs.

This latter report, being the report of Mr. Wilson's
Secretary and of the experienced merchant, must be considered the report emanating from the brains of the commission.

The report of the Lieut.-Governor's Secretary, of the
concurring Baboo and of the Rev. Mr. Sale may be read
as Mr. Grant's last manifesto against the planters.

It may be thought proper, however, that we should
make a few observations upon the Lieut.-Governor's
report.

To pursue it through its 190 paragraphs, and to cor-

planting and planters, and fomented a bad feeling on the part of the
Ryots towards the planters in every way in his power. I am aware that
Mr. Bomwetsch has denied having done so, but that gentleman's memory
must be rather treacherous." But Mr. Seton Karr, however, has managed
to make Mr. Sale's absolving paragraph, as damnatory as a Scotch verdict
of " not proven" to the whole body. He says—
" 130. In our opinion it is extremely unreasonable to attribute the
sudden failure of an unsound system, which had grown up silently for
years, *to the officials or Missionaries who told the people, that they
were free agents.* If it could be said with truth that greased cartridges
were only the proximate cause of a rebellion which had been silently
gathering for years, it may be said with even more truth that *written or
spoken words, widely circulated, and only pointing out to the Ryot what
was perfectly correct in all essentials,* namely, that it was optional with
them to take advances or to refuse them—to sow indigo or not to sow it—
were only the proximate cause of the extensive refusal to cultivate during
this season."
* Paragraphs 69 and 70. These paragraphs are the portions which
contain the summary of the relations between the planters and the
Ryots.
† "I further dissent from the language and tone of the Report, even
as to those points the truth of which I do not dispute, for the reason that
the language and tone tend to give a colouring and to lead to conclusions
not proved from the facts."

rect its errors by proofs, would, of course, be impractic--
able ; not on account of the difficulty of the writing, but
on account of the grievous severity of the reading. We
must content ourselves with skipping from blunder to
blunder with cursory comment, with cropping off an occasional tall audacity, and with pointing, from time to time,
to some salient manifestation of ignorance.

The first point which strikes a reader accustomed to
such documents is the contrast which this paper presents
to others that have proceeded from similar quarters not
later than five years ago. If a civilian planter-hater,
with a Governor behind him, preferment in front, and a
Baboo in his company, had, five years ago, undertaken
to concoct an arraignment against the British settlers in
the Mofussil, we should unquestionably have had a full
repetition of all the calumnies which have been disproved
and reproduced any time these last thirty years ; which
Governor-Generals and the most eminent natives have
always denounced as slanders, after strict official and
personal inquiry, but which have always reappeared with
an infamous immortality from some German Missionary,
or from some discontented policeman, or from some effete
and querulous civilian, or from some boy - magistrate
shaping his reports in such form as may make them
acceptable in high quarters. Publicity, however, may
we hope also, Christian principle? have literally forced
Mr. Grant's commissioners to withdraw from this old
ground, and to content themselves with putting real facts
in the most obnoxious point of view, " giving a colouring," as one of the protesting commissioners says, " by
language and tone, and leading to conclusions not proved
by the facts."

All this was not for want of careful inquiry. The

commissioners went back for thirty years. Every one who had a story to tell, or who even could say he had heard of such stories, was entreated to come forward. The Missionary and the Baboo were doubtless astonished to find that there was not even a vestige of foundation to be discovered for those charges of murder, rape, and arson, which other members of their classes have been so glibly repeating for the last fifty years, and which have passed rapidly, not only over India, but also over England, to use the words of this report, "in written or spoken words widely circulated."

After a thirty years' search after these "rapes," the commission is obliged to report—for the evidence was taken in public—as follows:—

" As to the outrages on women, which, more than any other act, might offend the prejudice and arouse the vindictiveness of a people notoriously sensitive as to the honour of their families, we are happy to declare that our most rigid inquiries could bring to light only one case of the kind. And when we came to examine into its foundation, as seriously affecting the character of one planter, and, through him, the body of planters in a whole district, or as affording any clue to the excitement of the past season, we discovered that there were reasonable grounds for supposing that no outrage on the person of the woman had ever taken place."

This is a curious paragraph. That outrages on women should offend the *prejudice* (!) of the natives is an odd way of speaking of such a crime. But that the commission's " *most rigid inquiries could bring to light only one case of the kind*" (in thirty years), in which one case " *no outrage on the person of the woman had ever taken place*" is certainly an example of ingenuity in making out a case of rape which could scarcely be rivalled by a prosecuting counsel in Ireland when Ireland enjoyed her own ancient pre-eminence in this class of accusations.

Of deaths arising from affrays there were proved to be forty-nine in thirty years, or three in two years, in a population of 20,000,000, these not being confined to indigo, but spreading over all causes of dispute in the Mofussil, and no planter ever having been implicated in any one of them.

As to " knocking down houses," the commission had been told by gentlemen that they " had seen places where houses had been," but " unless they could fathom the origin of all desertions, they could not take upon themselves to pronounce that houses had been wantonly knocked down by the planters." We recommend the President and his two assenting commissioners to take a tour in England and Wales, and make the same remark upon Caernarvon Castle, or the mound of Old Sarum, or the deserted old farm-houses in the fens, whence the farmers have moved up to the wolds, or upon those houses at the corner of Stamford Street, Blackfriars, or upon any deserted mud cottages (for such are the " homesteads " here spoken of), which they may see in their tour.*

* Here is a history of the principal case relied upon by the President, and the Missionary, and the Baboo. In occurs in the evidence of Mr. Larmour:—

Mr. Fergusson.] Q. Ameer Mullick, of Khanpore, was examined by this commission on the 2nd June. Have you read his evidence of your people having knocked down and plundered his house, and do you wish to give any explanation thereof?

A. Shortly after assuming the management of the Katgarrah concern, numerous petitions were presented to me at Mulnauth, from the Ryots of Barrakapore village, complaining to the effect that Ameer Mullick had collected a number of dacoits [thieves] and settled them adjoining his own house. Two of these petitions appeared to be exceedingly

We wonder whether, if a commission of indigo planters, and tea planters, and cotton growers, and silk filature owners, had been appointed to inquire into the conduct of the Civil Service and the condition of the salt Ryots, "the poorest labourers in all Bengal," and the opium Ryots, they could have conscientiously reported such a total absence of crime as this commission has been compelled to confess, and what they would have said about the salt Ryots "accounted for as carried off by tigers."

truthful, and stated that Ameer Mullick's gang had hitherto committed robberies at a distance, but of late they robbed the houses of the Ryots in Barrakapore: these petitions were forwarded by me to the magistrate of Nuddea, with the request that he would institute an inquiry into what was stated in these petitions. He ordered the police to make a local investigation, and at the time they went to Barrakapore to carry out this investigation, a robbery had been committed at Kotechandpore, in Zillah Jessore, the police of Jessore tracing the property to Barrakapore, where twelve of the gang were seized: four of them were convicted and sentenced to five years' imprisonment by the late Judge of Jessore, *now President of the present commission.* From the time of the seizure of this gang, Ameer Mullick absconded from Barrakapore, and did not return there again, except on the sly. My people had nothing to do whatever with the destruction of his house: it being left uninhabited, it very soon went to wreck and ruin, and I believe there was not a Ryot in the village, owing to what they had suffered from him and his gang, but were glad to pull at the straw and bamboos belonging to his house.

Mr. Seton Karr.] Q. Was any report made to the magistrate, the commissioner, or other authority, to the effect that one of the sons of Ameer Mullick harboured these criminals, though evidence was not forthcoming against him?

A. I remember the fact of Jalla Mullick, son of Ameer Mullick, being an outlaw, and the police after him for several months after the robbery at Kotechandpore.

Mr. Sale.] Q. What are we to understand by Jalla Mullick being an outlaw?

A. That the police of Jessore and Kishnaghur were in search of him all over the country.

Q. You spoke of the Ryots as wishing to have a pull at the bamboos of Ameer Mullick's house; did he not live in a pukka house?

A. No; the house in which he resided I have always understood to be a cutcha [mud] house, having two small pukka [brick] rooms on each side of the entrance to his compound.

Quite sure we are, that if they could have done this truly they would not have done it so grudgingly. Alas! they would have had evidence of a very different character to record to that which we here find, gathered alike from the "nobility" and from the refuse of India, and, in many instances, unfairly epitomized.

Mr. Seton Karr would seem to be labouring under an impression, that, in point of fact, his report must be a failure, and that it could not but be a great disappointment to Mr. Grant to find that, after calling him forth to curse his enemies, behold, he was going very near to bless them. However, we shall see presently, that although his premises failed him, this accident made no great difference in his conclusions.

Take the instance of paragraph 81, where Mr. Seton Karr quietly assumes a proposition contradicted by the evidence before him,* and draws a conclusion which is

---

* Mr. Larmour had been asked whether indigo was a remunerative crop. Mr. Larmour produced his books, and gave the following answer :—

A. That depends entirely on the season. In the last season, at the Mulnauth factory, the average return per beegah paid to the Ryots was 14 bundles per beegah. Upwards of 100 Ryots cut more than 20 bundles per beegah; 237 Ryots cleared off their advances and debt to the factory, and received *fazil*, or excess-payments. The return of 20 bundles per beegah pays a Ryot well, apart from the indigo seed which he also gets from the stumps. [Mr. Larmour here filed a paper in English, referring to the books in original, which he also filed.]

Even in their own report they say—"It is urged that it has still been found comparatively easy to satisfy the Ryot, and to keep him contented and faithful to his engagements, by the grant of what have been termed collateral advantages ; and that even with the above disadvantages several Ryots, *working honestly and faithfully, have cleared their advances, and received large payments in excess. This last averment is quite true.*" Do the Commissioners then mean to confine their sympathy and protection to those Ryots who do not "work honestly and faithfully," and therefore do not make a profit. It is but too manifest that they do, but it would have been more manly to have stated the fact.

in the teeth of the testimony of a cloud of witnesses. Civilians and planters, and the two most eminent natives of modern days, are for once consistent in flat contradiction to Mr. Seton Karr. The evidence of the natives upon this question was derived from personal experience, and was quoted by us a few pages back, and the matter is the gist of the matter upon which Mr. Seton Karr had passed so many days, and had taken so much evidence.   Here is the paragraph :—

" Conflicting statements have been made as to whether " there is or there is not a perceptible difference in the " condition of the Ryots who grow indigo, compared " with those who do not grow it.   Seeing *that it is not* " *to be contravened that the majority of Ryots derive no* " *profit, but a loss,* from indigo, and that many Ryots " in the greater part of Hooghly and Baraset, as well as " those on Mr. Morell's estate in Backergunge and in " other parts of that district, have grown rich and " wealthy, without this kind of cultivation, *we do not* " *discover any particular difference to be perceptible in* " *favour of Ryots who are cultivators of indigo.*"

This is as if Mr. Seton Karr had said, " Brewing cannot be a profitable trade ; because the late Mr. Rothschild made a large fortune, and he was never known to brew a butt of beer in his life."

But who will the people of England believe?   Rammohun Roy and Dwarkanauth Tagore, and the magistrate of Dacca, and the Governor-General, Lord William Bentinck, and Sir Charles Metcalfe, whose testimony we have already cited,[*] and the commissioner of Morabadad (Mr. Boldero), who says,[†] " So far as my experience

* Ante p. 18.
† " Conduct of Europeans in India," p. 181.

goes, and it is founded on a residence of six years in a district filled with indigo planters, I have found the lower classes of the natives better clothed, richer, and more industrious, in the neighbourhood of the factories, than those at a distance from them;" and Mr. Mills, the magistrate of Pubnah, who says, " It must be observed, that the condition of the Ryots has been greatly improved since the introduction of indigo in the Mofussil;" and the witnesses who gave evidence to the same effect before the Committee of the House of Lords which sat on the affairs of the East India Company in 1830; and Mr. Harris, who had been an indigo planter in India, and who stated that " their (the Ryots') better condition in the districts where indigo was chiefly cultivated, enabled them to keep a greater number of bullocks for their ploughs, and the ground was better cultivated as they improved in means;" will the people of England believe, we ask, this body of unbiassed testimony, or will they believe Mr. Grant's Secretary, reporting in contradiction to the evidence before him?

But let us proceed to other accusations. The President of this commission says—

" Another inequality is this : the planter, on a fair cal-" culation, looks to a return of two seers of dye from ten " bundles of plant, which is the fair average of one " beegah.   Two seers would sell for ten rupees, when in-" digo is selling at 200 rupees a maund.   But the return " from the same ten bundles to the Ryot could not be " more than two rupees and eight annas, at four bundles " the rupee.

" Thus the planter would look *to derive from the contract* " about four times the profit which could ever fall to the " Ryot."

I

What does any commercial man think of a trade being subjected to the intermeddling of such people as these ? The data assumed are false in fact, as the evidence before them shewed, for nothing is more variable than the yield of dye from the same bulk of plant. But if they were true, as they are false, what shall we say of a commission which makes calculations based upon the assumption that the raw material and the manufactured article are the same profit-bearing article ? What would the Liverpool cotton merchant and the Manchester manufacturer say if the Board of Trade were to send down some wiseacre to them, who should attempt to convince the Liverpool merchant that he was an ill-used man, because he was selling cotton for sixpence a pound, which the Manchester manufacturer sold *for twenty shillings a pound,* or 4000 per cent. " profit," when worked up into book-muslins ? What would the Manchester manufacturer say if this great political economist should attempt to convince him that he was a scoundrel for not allowing more of the cost of the manufactured article to the seller of the raw material ? What would they do ?—they would unite to shut up such a brainless meddler in some neighbouring lunatic asylum.

This really would seem to be penned by the same hand which insists that the planter has no capital but his vats and his credits, and that the Ryot who sows with another man's seed, who is paid beforehand for his labour, and who has bought his bullocks with the factory money, is the capitalist who in " capital" exceeds all others in the Mofussil.*

* " I must notice another misdescription in the memorial. The commercial dispute in question is designated a dispute between capital and labour."—*Mr. Grant's Minute.* Poor Mr. Grant actually does not know that when the terms " capital and labour " are thus used,

Surely, after this exhibition of crass and insensate ignorance, no one would follow us in any further examination of Mr. Seton Karr's notions of prices and profits.
The Ryot sells leaves and the indigo factor sells indigo.
If he would apply his measure of profits to the opium
Ryot, who yields ready-manufactured opium, and not
poppies, at 3s 6d a pound, which Mr. Grant sells again
at 20s a pound, or to the salt Ryot, who yields ready-
manufactured salt at seven annas, or tenpence halfpenny
a maund, of 84 pounds, which Government sells again at
three rupees twelve annas, or 7s 6d per maund, there
might be something practical in his deductions.

Let us go at once, then, to the " recommendations" of
these three gentlemen.

First, let us put aside a string of recommendations,
either unnecessary or worthless, addressed to the planters ;
for although no class is more 'attentive to good counsel
from friendly and well-informed men, the planters do not
hope to obtain such counsel from the numerical majority
of this commission. The paragraphs which are offered
" by way of suggestion and advice" from men who are
the mere nominees of those who have been the authors of
our ruin, and who are bitter enemies, we reject as an im-
pertinence.

The suggestions of the President of this commission
are : —

1st. That the position of honorary magistrate should
never be conferred upon an indigo planter.

The indigo planters never desired this position. It

---

people of any information on such subjects take for granted that labour
has its necessarily adhering qualities of capital, and is thus far, as much
capital as money itself. Capital is nothing but hoarded labour. We
have not space here to teach Mr. Grant the distinctions between fixed
and floating capital.

was forced upon them by the Government, then in its agony, and will be attempted to be forced upon them again when the income tax comes to be levied. What the planters have complained of was the insulting manner in which these commissions were all withdrawn, without one case of misconduct proved, and with the degradation thus inflicted in the eyes of the Ryots. The planter had more power in his own court of arbitration, deciding the disputes of his neighbours, and freely obeyed by them, than he had by reason of any magisterial authority.

2dly. The President recommends that sub-divisions should be still more multiplied, vouching the good effect of this measure in Baraset under Mr. Eden!

Let us here interject a few lines about this Mr. Eden. It is not given to us to commence our task with—

" Musa mihi causas memora,"

but it is necessary in order to set our case before the public that we should state the fact that the whole of this state of confusion in the social and commercial relations of Bengal began in the first instance with acts of unprovoked hostility by the Honourable Ashley Eden; who had been at an earlier period of his career upon excellent terms with the planters within his district.

If any of our readers would desire to see a specimen of the spirit which actuates this gentleman, we submit to him some extracts from Mr. Eden's evidence given before the Commissioners and which we have printed in the Appendix to this pamphlet. When we read the savage-like disappointment that he could not try in a Native Court the European, who, with the sympathy of the bystanders, was acquitted by the Supreme Court of

Calcutta, we think of this man's history and we think of the probability of his yet having a white man's fate in his hands, and we literally shudder. To the reader of Mr. Eden's evidence we beg to explain, that when Mr. Eden says "If the Native Courts are good enough for Natives, they are good enough for Europeans," he by no means means that they are good enough for Mr. Eden. If this were proposed, he would soon find out that a Native Court might be an impartial Court as towards natives, but a very fatal Court as towards Europeans, whether planter or civilian.

3dly. It is recommended that the police should receive higher wages; the evidence being that the higher their wages, the greater men they are, and the greater bribes they expect. But as the Commissioners complacently say, "A reform of corruption so long discussed and so fully laid bare must be—" What? Immediate?—No! Earnestly and promptly accomplished?—No! "Must be—*a work of time!*"

4thly. With reference to a great ground of complaint brought by "large and influential Zemindars," of an Act which withdraws from them the power of compelling the attendance of their tenants for the adjustment of their rents, or for any other purpose,* the Commissioners recommend, not that the right should be restored, but that "the working of the Act"—that is, the working of the absence of a right—"should be very carefully watched!"

5thly. The Commissioners see no use in any Special Indigo Commissioner to act as moderator between planters and Ryots.

Mr. Temple places great stress upon the necessity of

---

* This is what the Commissioners call "kidnapping" when the old feudal right was exercised by British leascholders of manors.

such an officer; and so should we if the nomination were not in the hands of such a man as Mr. J. P. Grant. As his instrument, a special commissioner would be a curse both to planter and to Ryot.

6thly. The Commissioners are of opinion that the interests of the planter do not imperatively demand any special protection. That is to say, that the planter has no right to ask for a summary process for enforcing his contracts, or recovering his crops, which are grown with his money.

This is throwing away the loosely-worn mask. At last we have found a little knot of people, numbering among them the Secretary to the Government of Bengal, who set their faces avowedly against cheap and summary justice, and advise the maintenance of long, expensive and ruinous suits. Mr. Grant has since indorsed this recommendation of his Secretary, and has referred the indigo manufacturers to the ordinary Civil Courts.

The English reader can have no adequate idea what a reference to the Civil Courts of India means. It sounds like an offer of justice on this side of the world; it carries the full smart of a mocking insult on the other side. When Mr. Seton Karr and Mr. John Peter Grant tell the indigo manufacturers that they have no right to cheap and speedy justice, and that the Civil Courts are good enough for them, as they are for other people, we must ask the English public to listen for a few seconds to testimony of what the Civil Courts in India really are.—

Some time ago attention in England was awakened in a spasmodic manner to the grotesque iniquity of the Indian judicial system—a natural result of a system formed by lawmakers and judges without legal education, and making laws and precedents by rule of thumb. Mr.

Campbell for the north, and Mr. Norton for the south of
India, laid bare the mystery ; and it was so funny that
the mirth of the public stifled its indignation. As Mr.
Seton Karr says that " the corruption of the police has
been so long discussed and so fully laid bare that its reform must be a work of time," so he and Mr. Grant probably think that the abuses of the Civil Courts have now
been proved to be so intolerable, that it is in every way
desirable that the Ryots and the planters should bear
them. That, at any rate, has been their declared intention, although that intention seems now likely to be
baulked. Be it remembered, however, that it is under
these men's heels our fortunes are now crunching ; and
the mere fact that we have hopes of being saved from
some of the tender mercies they had in store for us, by no
means diminishes the urgency of our cry to be delivered
altogether from their power.

The Civil Courts, to which Mr. Grant insists that the
most trifling indigo causes ought to be confined, afford a
perpetuity of litigation ; and, until Mr. Grant established
a rule by which the judgments range all on one side, they
provided also the greatest possible uncertainty of event,
from the technicalities of the procedure.

For a question of 40*s* there may be in Bengal five
appeals, and perhaps five times five trials.

This will not be believed, and we must really ask the
indulgence of a hearing for two or three actual cases, as
cited by Mr. Norton from the authorised Reports.

Mr. Norton cites his cases for the purpose, among
other objects, of attacking the competency of the civilians
to act as judges. Such is not our purpose. We cite
them to shew that judges are not removed in India
merely on account of judicial incompetency. We would

rather take our chance of such judges as may fall to our lot, than have the very worst weeded out for our use, and instructed to decide against us. Mr. Norton says—

" I proceed at once to the Reports, premising only that since their publication these disclosures have frequently become the topic of conversation and wonder among reflecting men, who are scarcely to be put aside by the remark which usually greets any one who ventures to bring a more than ordinarily atrocious judgment to the notice of any of the ' Service '—' Oh, but that judge is mad !' or ' He is an idiot !' or ' He drinks !' although politeness forbids one to put the question which naturally suggests itself, ' Why is such a man permitted to remain on the Bench ?' "

" 47 of 1851, vol. 3, p. 135.—Case No. 47 of 1851. An appeal from the decision of Mr. ——,* C. Judge of Guntoor (formerly Judge of the Sudder). This was a suit for the recovery of a piece of ground of the value of 40 rupees (£4.) It was tried over three times; and at the date of the Report was sent back by the Sudder for a fourth trial, from which it is to be remembered there might possibly be a further appeal. The Courts below had omitted to record points (in accordance with the Regulation) for the parties to prove; and both the District Moonsiff and the Civil Judge *had neglected to notice the plea urged by the Defendants that they had been in possession for 40 years.*"

" No. 56 of 1851, vol. 3, p. 155.—No. 56 of 1851 is

---

* Mr. Norton gives the names. We omit them to avoid giving pain to any of the gentlemen whose decisions are cited.

amusing.   It is an appeal from a decision of Mr. ——,
C. Judge of Salem.

"The Plaintiff sued for 125 rupees, money advanced to Defendant
under a contract for the supply of oil.   Defendant pleaded that he had
been always ready and willing to fulfil his contract, but had been prevented by the Plaintiff.

"The Moonsiff who originally tried the case disbelieved the Plaintiff's
evidence, and gave the Defendant a verdict.

"The Plaintiff appealed to the C. Judge, who reversed the Moonsiff's
decree.

"The Defendant appealed to the Sudder, who remanded the suit;
making the following observations:—'The Court of Sudder Adawlut
'observe that the C. Judge has evidently mistaken the object for which
'the suit was brought.   It was instituted for the recovery of 125 rupees,
'advanced by the Plaintiff to the Defendant; and not, as would seem to
'be the impression of the C. Judge, *for a quantity of oil!*'

" No. 4 of 1847, p. 36, vol. 1, is a short but instructive case.

"The suit was originally brought for a piece of ground of the value
of 15 rupees (£1. 10s) and a house of the value of 40 rupees (£4.), and
for an 'injunction to have a wall built.'   This case was tried *five*
times; and the Sudder, ' as at present constituted,' over-ruled their
predecessors."

" No. 25 of 1847, p. 46, vol. 1. —This was a Special
Appeal from the decision of Mr. —— (afterwards a Judge
of the Sudder Court).

" It was tried *six* times, although the Court of Sudder are at last
' *clearly of opinion that this suit is barred by the Statute of Limitations.*' ! ! !

" And the case is further instructive because the lower
Courts gave a verdict for the plaintiff, who sued as heir
against a personal representative, *without enquiring
whether he was heir, or if defendant had possessed himself
of assets ! ! !*

" No. 2 of 1849, p. 105, vol. 1.—This is a shocking
case.   It is from the decision of Mr. —— —, Actg. Asst.
Judge of the Adawlut Court of Malabar.   The amount

in dispute was small : the amount of litigation frightful. It appears to have extended over a period from 1825 to 1840. *It was tried over five times,* besides a considerable amount of petitioning ; and after all it turns out to be barred by the Statute of Limitations.

" No. 20 of 1848, p. 119, vol. 1.—This is a Special Appeal from a decision of Mr. ——, C. Judge of Rajahmundry.

" Plaintiff's estate had been put up and sold by the Government for arrears of Kist ; a proceeding which, according to the law, satisfies the Government claim. And the Proprietor is expressly empowered, by Sec. 18 of Reg. 28 of 1802, in such an event to sue his tenants for any arrears of rent due by them. The Plaintiff brought his action to recover the sum of Rupees 45-12-10 (£4. 10s) the amount of rent due to him by the Defendant, his tenant. The Sub-Judge gave him a verdict, which the Civil Judge reversed on appeal. The Plaintiff thereupon appealed to the Sudder, who naturally reversed the decree of the Civil Judge."

" Special Appeal Petition, No. 19 of 1850, p. 5, vol. 2. —This was a suit for the recovery of rent. Defendant pleaded *that he had not occupied the premises.* Both the lower Courts adjudged him to pay the rent *without deciding that issue or taking any evidence upon it.* The SUDDER remands it for a *third trial.*"

" No. 13 of 1840, vol. 2, p. 78.—This is a Special Appeal from a decision of Mr. ——, C. Judge of Trichinopoly.

" It was brought for the recovery of a piece of ground of the value of 3 Rupees (6s). It has been tried three times, and remanded for a fourth trial. The Defendants had been in ' undisturbed possession of ' the land for a lengthened period.' The Plaintiff proved his purchase from a *third* party ; but the ' title of that party to the land not being ' satisfactorily established,' the C. Judge reversed the decree of the Sudder Ameen in Plaintiff's favour ; but the investigation was carried on in such a way that the Sudder declared it ' impossible from the

'evidence before them to arrive at any just or satisfactory conclusion as
'to which party the land under litigation rightfully belongs.'

" So here are four trials about a piece of land of the
value of six shillings."

" No. 38 of 1850, vol. 2, p. 89.—A Special Appeal
against the decision of Mr. ——, C. Judge of Cud-
dapah.

"This is a case for the recovery of Rupees 12-10 damages, in consequence of an interference of Defendants with the exercise of certain
privileges of Plaintiff's deceased father.   The case has occupied from
1845 to 1850.   It has been already tried three times, and is now to
begin again."

" No. 63 of 1848, vol. 2, p. 94.—This is a Special
Appeal from a decision of Mr. ——, Acting C. Judge
of Trichinopoly.   *When* this suit was instituted does not
appear, further than that it was *before* 1842.   It was a
simple question of fact.   It has been *tried eight times.*"

Bad enough that such stupidity as is here recorded
should remain upon the judgment-seat; but these
faults do not incur deprivation of authority.   Judicial
officers may commit these blunders and remain.   It is
only if they dare to put in force an Act of Council,
or abide by the laws of evidence, or do right between
man and man in a way which Mr. Grant dislikes, that
they become obnoxious to the absolute power of removal
exercised by the Governor.   We agree with Mr. Norton
that the judges of whom he complains are not desirable
upon the bench; for ignorance works injustice as well as
subserviency or partiality; but we should be sorry to see
even these judges removed by a secret and irresponsible
mandate, without public accusation, or public inquiry, or

a possibility of public explanation or defence, as the judicial officers in the Mofussil were by Mr. Grant.

The direct object of our quotations, however, was to shew, not the ignorance of the civilian judges, but the sort of Courts to which Mr. Grant and Mr. Seton Karr solemnly decided that all indigo cases should be confined. The reader will have observed that nearly all these cases, for trifling sums, have been tried *from three to eight times;* and, moreover, that they had been in litigation for many years.*

The facts we have proved are so monstrous, that we cannot still help fearing, that, although they are so notorious in India, conceded by every one there, and resting upon the published records of the Courts, the English public will think we are overstating our case, and say that such things cannot be. All we can say is, here are our proofs—the authorised Reports of the Courts themselves. Now these are the Courts to which Mr. Grant and his Secretary, when the question was brought before them for an expression of opinion, deliberately determined that the jurisdiction over contracts for growing indigo ought to be confined. We ask, is it not more cruel to leave such a man in powe over us, even than to leave upon the bench the blundering judges who make the Courts of India a farce?

We confine our statement to our own indigo contracts because indigo is our business, and because the number

---

* It will be answered that some reform in the procedure has recently taken place. The answer is ridiculous. The reform is like the reform in Chancery; a good thing as far as it goes, but that is all. You may still have five appeals, and a dozen trials, and twenty years of litigation about a beegah of indigo stalks.

of our contracts is so great; and also because the knowledge that the Civil Courts afford no practical remedy
increases our risks, and renders it impossible to give the
cultivator so much for his produce, as we could give him
if we were buying a security instead of a hope. But
the argument is not less strong in favour of a summary
law of contract for all classes, natives as well as English.*

Evidence is scattered about in reams, proving to all

---

* It is to such courts that at this moment, when indigo contracts and
rents are alike repudiated, planters and Zemindars are referred by Mr.
Grant. In the district of Kishnagur, with 1,500,000 inhabitants, there
are upwards of 100,000 parties holding indigo contracts, and about
300,000 who pay, or should pay, rent. Deducting holidays, there are
not 200 working days of six hours in the year. Suppose every case to
occupy two hours, though frequently one takes as many days, 600 years
would be required to hear the complaints, and three times that time to
decide the appeals. Then the expense of suing on a contract to recover
10 to 16 rupees would be about as under :—

	Rs.	A.	Pie.
Stamp for Mooktearnamah	0	8	0
„ for petition with affixes, if short, say . .	2	0	0
if long, 3r. to 5r.			
„ for tendering witnesses, say four at 8 annas .	2	0	0
„ for reply to defendant's pleas	2	0	0
„ for peons fees for giving notice to defendant .	1	4	0
Cost of summoning witnesses, at 12 annas . . .	3	0	0
Vakeels' fees ·	2	0	0
Mohurrir for writing, etc.	1	0	0
	13	12	0

To this add :—	Rs.	A.	Pie.			
Expense of sending a servant to the Court to						
produce books, say	2	8	0			
Diet money to witnesses, at 1 rupee . .	4	0	0			
Sundry expenses for sending to station during						
3 or 4 months, while suit is pending . .	2	0	0			
Court Mohurrir, for writing evidence, say						
8 annas each witness	2	0	0			
				10	8	0
			Rs.	24	4	0

who can hear that the practical denial of legal redress
raises the rate of interest in the Mofussil* to more than
£100. per cent. per annum among those native dealers
with whom every native deals; that even this rate will
not cover the risk; and that the want of capital consequent upon insecurity keeps the farmer poor and wretched.
All this has been proved; for it seems this self-evident
necessary law of political economy required to be proved
before this Commission. But all in vain. Mr. Seton
Karr, representing the Lieutenant-Governor's classical
animosity to the British settler; the Baboo, representing
the short-sighted love of shirks and evasions of the class

* See the evidence of Mr. MacNair before the Colonization Committee, 1858, upon this point.
" 2001. *Mr. Willoughby.*] Do you mean the advance of funds?—
Yes, to native cultivators. In India, where the system of advance pre-
vails to such an extent, where the native cultivators are generally so
poor, they cannot provide seed for their lands, or engage to deliver any
produce, without previously obtaining a considerable advance, generally
equal to the value of the produce, *a good law of contract is much required for all classes, English and natives.* Government found it
necessary to have stringent laws of contract for their OWN OPIUM AD-
VANCES; and if they would extend that law to all parties, Europeans and
natives, it would save a great deal of litigation and cases of affrays. The
present law of complaining before the Civil Courts is so expensive and
tedious, it is, in fact, an encouragement to ill-disposed people to break
their contracts; it is a very common thing for small natives who save
or have a little money, to lend it or make advances to natives upon
their crops; *most of them are ruined from not being able to recover
their advances, which is the sole cause why so very exorbitant rates are
taken by native dealers.* These high rates bear hard upon the poor
cultivators, and is the principal cause of their poverty. It seems to be
a popular proposition of Government to put all their subjects upon the
same footing, and under the same laws; *but they claim to keep their
own servants of every grade, from the highest to the lowest, exempt
from these laws, and also have different laws of contract for their own
opium and salt advances.*" What would Mr. Karr and Mr. Grant say
if it were proposed to take away their summary jurisdiction over the
Government salt and opium Ryots? They would say, and would say
truly, that it was a proposition to destroy an annual seven millions of
public revenue.

of Ryots; and the Missionary, representing we know not what, determine that there shall be no cheap and speedy law of contracts in India, lest the planters should get justice, and that all India shall have long expensive suits, lest the British settler should grow up to over-shadow the civilian.

Mr. Temple must have laughed much at his colleagues' notions of capital and labour, and at their ideas of the mode of judging the profit upon manufactured articles, by getting at the price of the raw material, and also at their imperviousness to the fact that the interest of money bears some relation to the security of the loan; but he must have laughed still more heartily at the clumsy notion of ruining a great interest by drowning them in law costs. Mr. Temple knows, that if the planters were so reckless and so wicked as to do against others what is done against them, they might, at the last desperate moment, clog all the courts of Bengal, and spread all over the land the devastation of that infamous law which is, and ever has been, the admitted reproach and opprobrium of our rule in India.

We were at first struck with wonder that there should be three men in India who could sign such a document as this; but we understand it all when we recognise in the last paragraphs polite recapitulations of Mr. Grant's own phrases, fresh from his Minute, and we remember that Mr. Seton Karr drew the Report, and that in all pro-bability the Baboo and the Missionary knew little of the technicalities of this question, and cared not to dispute with a judge upon the efficiency of his own courts.

This is all. This is all which Mr. Karr and his two

coadjutors recommend. No injunctions against perwannahs. No recommendations to Governors not to inter-
meddle between buyers and sellers. No disapproval of
proclamations to cultivators absolving them from their
contracts. No suggestion to State officers to let commerce and trade alone. They recommend only more
magistrates, whom Mr. Grant shall appoint and remove;
more pay to Mr. Grant's corrupt police; and more suits,
which shall be interminable, or over which Mr. Grant
shall have absolute dominion. Is not this a Report worthy
of the wisdom and the impartiality of the source whence
it proceeds!

Let us now turn for a moment to the separate Report
made by Mr. Temple and Mr. Fergusson.

We cannot of course, expect from Mr. Temple, all civilian as he is, more than that his class instincts should be
controlled by his general good sense and by his higher
intelligence. We must not seek from him admissions of
that traditionary jealousy which the Civil Service have
always entertained for a class of whom Dwarkanauth
Tagore could publicly say, that they were more valuable
to India than the Civil Service. No civilian would just
now admit this. We must be content to mark the hostile
instincts of the Civil Service in the public records of their
offices, in the acts of their Government, in the whole con-
stitution of Indian society, in the public crimes whereof
we now impeach Mr. J. P. Grant, and in the ruin of
" the mainstay and chief hope of stability of British
power in the East." We must not expect Mr. Temple to
tell us, that while the British House of Commons have
been sitting in anxious deliberation to devise means of

scattering over the rural districts of India, Europeans,
whose skill, energy, and capital, may brace together in
industrious force that relaxed and feeble population,* the
fanatical members of the Civil Service have been endeavouring to accomplish an exactly opposite task.   Just as
Mr. Temple is more clever and more keen than his colleagues, so is he more skilful to avoid placing the weak-
nesses of his caste in a conspicuous light.

The way at this moment to quiet India is to bring a
great criminal to justice.   Shocking as it may be to the
notions of civilians, who think it little less than impiety
to lay a hand upon a member of the White Brahmin caste,
there is no other remedy even for state crimes but punishment.   In England, if a Minister had interfered with the
course of justice as Mr. J. P. Grant has done, dismissing
magistrates according to his will, and with the avowed intention of obtaining a certain class of decisions; circulating pattern decisions to magistrates whose bread hung
upon his breath, that Minister would have been punished.
There is no other real remedy for the ruin which is now
rising in India.   For the crimes of stirring up debtors
against their creditors, and of violently detorting the
course of justice, are not crimes whose consequences can
be neutralized by a mere law.   You cannot prevent robberies or murders by enacting that henceforth there shall
be no robberies and no murders – they are crimes which
must be put down by punishment.   It is not to be endured,
that in a country where all men are supposed to have equal
rights, a Minister should do these things, and should then

---

* " The Ryot works three hours a day upon an average."—*Mr.
Larmour's Evidence.*

K

point to the disruption of that social order which it was his duty to maintain, and to say, " I thought it right to do this." The only remedy for such crimes is inquiry, impeachment, and punishment.

Nothing of this shall we find in Mr. Temple's Report. Mr. Temple thinks that the corruption of the police is " at the root of the matter." This is to a certain extent true: but *now* the police are not *only* corrupt. They know now which side they may safely abuse. The police take their tone from their masters. When the Lieutenant-Governor stamps his bias so unquestionably upon the judge, there can be little surprise that it should be seen in operation a stage lower down. It has been deposed by Mr. Dalrymple, that bodies of police do vary according to the character of the magistrate, and that there are actually some active magistrates who have brought their police to such perfection, that it is scarcely possible to bribe them. If a judge may coerce his constabulary to honesty, or at least to caution, how prompt will they be to lend their assistance against any class he may be thought to dislike.

Nevertheless, as a general proposition, it is true that the corruption of the Government police is a great difficulty—a difficulty to which, when are superadded, the whole power of the Government exerted to produce a strike, a despotic minister shuffling the judges and opening the gaols, and the total negation of all civil remedy for the enforcement of contracts, the contest becomes hopeless indeed.

Mr. Temple does not, however, leave us with a barren recommendation to change the nature of our own native servants and of the Government police. He stands by

his order as he can; but he slips away from the side of
Mr. Seton Karr when that gentleman adopts too literally
the notion of Mr. Grant, his principal, proposing to try
the property in bundles of indigo plant by " equity suits."
Mr. Temple reports, as we have already said, in favour
of a Summary Process Act.*

* It is important that the reader should have before him the principal
arguments with which Mr. Temple and Mr. Fergusson combat the
proposition of Mr. Seton Karr to leave the planters remediless to their
fate:—

" The precarious nature of the crop in Lower Bengal, the critical emergencies which arise in the cultivation of indigo, have been shewn in the
Report. Similar emergencies may arise even in the manufacture. Thus
it is possible, and does actually happen, that the planter is involved in
sudden difficulties through no fault of his own. His Ryots may have
taken advances, and then refuse to sow; or they may delay to sow within
a few hours, during which alone the sowing for a season's crop will be
possible. There is hardly any other product, the culture of which is
liable to such a crisis as this. Then in the midst of the manufacturing
season the hired labourer may absent himself, or, contrary to agreement,
strike for higher wages. The Ryot (especially if as suggested he received
a considerable payment, whether a crop is cut or not) may refuse to
exert himself in the case of inundation or destructive accidents. Now it
appears to us *that wherever the conduct of any business is from its nature
critical ; wherever breach of contract would, if not immediately redressed,
cause irreparable loss or inconvenience to the opposite party ; the policy
of the law has been to render such breach of contract liable to criminal
penalties.* Such has been the principle followed in the case of domestic
servants, of workmen, of railway labourers, and, as we understand, in the
case of coffee planters ; and recently this appears to have been the
principle which guided the Legislature in passing the Summary and
Temporary Act for indigo cultivation during the season of 1860. If
the principle has been correctly described above, then we submit that it
applies in the cultivation and manufacture of indigo cultivation as much
as to any case whatever. Indeed, we believe that in none of the cases
in which the principle has been sanctioned, is the business more critical,
or the inconvenience more immediate, or the loss more difficult of repa-
ration, than in the case of indigo cultivation.

" We would therefore recommend that the Act of XI. of 1860, rendering breaches of contract to cultivate indigo criminally punishable by the
magistrate, might be made permanent, with certain modifications. And
we would extend it to breaches of contract to manufacture indigo, so
that a Ryot who has engaged to cultivate, or a labourer who has

Mr. Temple also recommends a registration of indigo contracts. This would be a very convenient course, if the planters could have any confidence in the governors

engaged to manufacture, may be by law compelled summarily to fulfil his engagement.

"It may be asked why should such criminal penalties be enacted to enforce contracts to cultivate indigo, when there is no such law for contracts to cultivate any other crop. To this we would reply, that, in the first place, with no other crop is the culture affected by such emergencies as with indigo. Rice or jute, or other products, do not, like indigo, need to be sown on the instant, after a particular shower. Such products are sown in the rainy season, and the sowings may be completed to-day, or to-morrow, or the next day, or the day after that. But with indigo the sowing must be completed within a few hours, or it may prove a failure. So it often happens with it in cutting. Much of the plant is grown on the river side. Frequently the river may be rising just as the plant is being cut. If there be the least delay, the crop may be damaged or destroyed by inundation.

"In the next place, with indigo the cultivation has to be arranged for, and the manufacture to be managed by the same capitalists. This is not the case with other produce generally. With an article like rice, the village banker may advance some money to the Ryot on the security of the crop, and the lender may take a part of the crop in payment ; but beyond the repayment of the loan he has no interest in the crop. If the Ryot fail to sow or to raise a crop, the banker will nevertheless sue the Ryot and recover his own with interest. But the indigo planter advances cash, not to trade in money and the interest thereof, but to ensure the delivery of a certain quantity of plant. It is in the *plant* that the planters' hopes centre. It is for *this* that he invests capital in building factories and maintains expensive establishments. If therefore, there be a failure of the plant, the planter loses not only the sums he has advanced (which may be of comparatively lesser consequence), but the season's profit, for the sake of which so much capital has been sunk, so much current expense incurred. If such a loss occur, it will be of little use to the planter to sue the Ryot for the recovery of advances. Such recovery would not cover more than a fraction of the damage sustained. It is evident, therefore, that the liabilities incurred by the indigo planter, and the stake held by him in the culture are not to be compared with the limited risk run by those who lend money to cultivators of land. We therefore confidently submit, that in this very respect the production of indigo is, in the nature of things, widely different from the case of any other product in Lower Bengal.

"Further, it may be said, if a law of this nature be enacted for indigo contracts, it may be equally required for silk contracts, and perhaps other similar contracts. Doubtless this is true. And if the just protection of the silk interest, or other interest similarly circumstanced with

placed over them. But when discussing this very subject,
Mr. Seton Karr insisted that the only plan consistent
with the dignity of the service would be, that the planter

indigo, should require a special contract law, such lawful assistance
might, we think, with good policy, be conceded.

"Lastly, although the practice of advances by indigo planters to
Ryots is not a desirable one, and might with advantage be discontinued,
still we apprehend that *as, by the custom of the country, nothing can be
done without cash advances, these will have to be continued.* Then, if
the planters should (as we hope they will) consent to grant the amount
of advances to the Ryot absolutely, whether the crop yield that value or
not, whereby the risk now borne by the Ryot will be transferred to the
planter ; then we observe that an ill-disposed Ryot will have a certain
degree of temptation to neglect his cultivation, being assured beforehand
of a fixed payment. Now this inevitable disadvantage, in a scheme that
is otherwise excellent, will be removed by a special law such as we recommend. If a Ryot shall try to abuse the advantage conceded to him,
the planter will have a real means of redress. And the consciousness of
this would, we believe, render planters more ready to make to the Ryot
those concessions which are so desirable.

"For all these reasons we recommend that a law like that of Act XI.
of 1860, be enacted for indigo contracts. We anticipate, that, under
the better system which must now be introduced, such a law will seldom
have to be actually enforced, and that numerous cases like those which
occurred in Kishnaghur district and which were much to be regretted,
would not occur in future. *The moral effect of such an enactment would
suffice, in ordinary times, to induce Ryots to fulfil their engagements,
and would give confidence to the planting interest, at a time when severe
sacrifices are demanded of it.*

"When a similar law was enacted in 1835, it did, we believe, work
well, and was approved by the Government of the time. *It was afterwards repealed,* because it was thought to operate prejudicially to the
Ryot. But with the improvements which we hope to see effected, the
Ryot will be in a good and independent position ; and there will be no
fear of the law pressing more hardly upon him that it does upon domestic servants, artificers and labourers.

"But if a law on the principle of Act XI. of 1860 be enacted, we do
not think that the taking of a cash advance, which is, by the present
law, the test of a contract having been made, would suit as a primary
condition in a permanent law. Such a provision would tend to render
permanent the vicious system of advances *which now pervades every
description of work, and every kind of transaction, whether it be the
Government manufacture of opium and salt, the making of indigo, and
indeed, every thing else.* The condition should be a regular contract to
cultivate, or a contract to manufacture. And measures should be taken
to ensure the contract being regular and *bond fide*."—*Report.*

and all his Ryots should journey off to the magistrate at a distance. Of course, as was explained to him, not a Ryot would go, and there would be no valid contracts. Or, probably, if the planter were to be earnest in attempting to entice his Ryots to go and have his contract registered, he would be charged by Mr. Grant with "kidnapping" them.

Mr. Temple also deals with another matter, which, seeing that Mr. Grant has so expounded the Act as to convey to the Ryots the impression that all their contracts are void, may well occasion some future trouble.

After stating his views as to registered contracts thus—

"We would then make the breach of a *registered con-*
"*tract to cultivate indigo* punishable by a magistrate, but
"not any other contract except a registered one. It would
"be very desirable to make the terms of such contracts
"explicit, so as to include the whole process of cultivating,
"from the ploughing to the cutting and delivery at the
"factory. We do not think that registration of agree-
"ments on the part of coolies to *manufacture* indigo
"would be necessary. We would, however, have breaches
"of such agreements punished by a magistrate, in the
"same manner as breaches of contract on the part of
"workmen or domestic servants."

Mr. Temple adds—

"While recommending a law prescribing criminal pe-
"nalties for the breach of registered contracts to culti-
"vate indigo; and while also admitting the great improve-
"ment made in the ordinary Civil procedure; we antici-
"pate that there will probably arise cases, or classes of

" cases, for which some special measures will be desirable.
" There are, we believe, in many indigo concerns, con-
" tracts made by Ryots previously to the present year,
" to cultivate indigo for various periods or terms of years
" not yet expired. Such contracts will probably be found
" to have been made by the Ryots according to the un-
" derstanding, at the time existing, of the relations be-
" tween the planter and the Ryot. In the present state
" of feeling among the people, it appears not impossible
" that some of these contracts might be disputed or repu-
" diated by the Ryot. Without attempting to form any
" opinion on the validity or otherwise of such contracts, a
" matter which must depend upon the merit of cases, we
" still think that the occurrence of such disputes should
" be watched. If in any district a considerable number
" of these contracts should be disputed, it would be very
" desirable to depute some competent and selected officers
" to try *promptly on the spot* any suits that might be
" brought, and to carry out their decisions with effect.
" The course to be pursued, however, should be well con-
" sidered, because the settlement of one case at the out-
" set might govern the decision of a great number of
" other cases."

Here comes the great kidnapping question—

" Act X. of 1859, which abolishes the power previously
" vested in a landlord of summoning his tenant for the
" payment of rent, has been much complained of by
" planters, as interfering with their manorial influence
" over the Ryot; and evidence on the point has been ten-
" dered. We admit the importance in many ways of pre-
" serving the influence of the landlord over his tenantry,

" but we must trust that whether they have the power of
" summoning vested in the law, or not, the landowners
" still exercise great influence. We do not wish to elevate
" the peasant at the expense of the upper class, but the
" peasant is entitled to a certain degree of protection.
" And many experienced men think that the additional
" protection afforded by the new law was really needed in
" Bengal. We do not see, moreover, how this law affects
" the planters more than other landlords, and on the whole
" we refrain from offering any recommendation on this
" head. We have done enough in drawing attention to
" the subject, and we hesitate, as at present informed, to
" do more.

" But now that indigo planters have become large
" landed proprietors, and indeed form a very important
" section in the landholding community, it is evident that
" the indigo interest has become bound up in the tenure of
" land."

Now arises the question of rent. The Report of Mr.
Temple and Mr. Fergusson continues—

" As the planters have, in common with other land-
" lords, been deprived of the power of summoning Ryots,
" we would venture to draw the attention of Government
" to the speedy recovery of rents. If power be taken
" from the landlord, it is the more necessary that the law
" should afford prompt redress. We know that attention
" was given to this point in the framing of Act XI. of
" 1860. And we trust that adequate machinery may be
" available for ensuring the expeditious recovery of rent,
" as the matter deeply affects the settlement of European
" capitalists in the interior."

Mr. Temple also gives advice to the planters, and we are sure it will be received in an amicable spirit. Mr. Temple's very judicious advice is to raise the price of the indigo plant to the Ryot. The only objection we have to offer to this recommendation is, that it was not necessary when it was available, for that we were just attempting to agree upon the terms; and that it is now rendered impracticable or unavailing by Mr. Grant's interference.

Just previous to Mr. Eden's perwannahs, when the Government took upon themselves to sponge out all the obligations of the Ryots to the planters, every indigo factor had become persuaded that the time had arrived when, in some way, the price of the indigo plant must be raised. Rice had risen; labour had risen (nearly cent per cent in a few years); the Government salt Ryots— poor wretches! — were literally starving; the opium Ryots were working for the prices they received when rice was one-half the present ruling prices. There was discontent everywhere. The indigo planters were a little a-head of other employers of labour, for they had doubled their wages and trebled their prices within thirty years, which was more than twice as much as the Government had done for its Ryots. But Government had their forced labour, and their summary laws, and the planters had no forced labour and no laws at all. The only question was, what concession should be made, and how it should be made? This was what was then agitating the Mofussil. The parties were cautiously scanning each other, as is the wont of bargain-making. This was the intention of one of the foremost, and as Mr. Temple rightly calls him, " one of the most eminent and experienced among the body of planters, Mr. James Forlong." We take the passage from Messrs. Temple and Fergusson's Report :—

" My own intention is to make a contract with the
" Ryots, of as simple a character as possible, to give each
" man a cash advance of two rupees a beegah, which, as
" he would have it for twelve months without interest,
" would be equal, at the lowest, to three rupees a beegah ;
" that the above two rupees should be given to the Ryot,
" on condition of his cultivating, irrespective of all risk to
" himself connected with the crop ; that whether there is
" a crop, or no crop at all, no portion of this money should
" be charged to him in any future account, thereby se-
" curing under any circumstances to the Ryot a reason-
" able remuneration for his labour, and for the rent of his
" land. *Eight bundles per beegah would pay off the
" first advance, and a Ryot, with ordinary luck and
" industry, might very easily secure a crop of double the
" amount. I would also abolish the charges for stamp,
" for carriage, for seed ; throwing really the risk of the
" crop upon the factory, and leaving a hope of a very
" liberal return to the cultivator."

Different factories were differently circumstanced. Many were already giving a rupee for four bundles. There were various arrangements as to carrying the plant. All these matters required much bargaining and adaptation to the desires of the Ryots. But all was coming to a compromise ; and as the Ryots could practically hold out, and the planters could not, things would

---

* Note in Report.—This is at the rate of one rupee per four bundles, which, at the present rate of price, is a fair price.

have righted themselves, as all such matters of bargain do right themselves.

Then it was that Mr. Grant was, unhappily, appointed to succeed Sir F. Halliday as Lieut.-Governor of Bengal ; and in a few hours it was believed that he united the two most disastrous crazes that a man in office can have in his head, and he brought them to bear upon this delicate conjuncture.   His acts have justified all men in concluding that he considers it his duty to vindicate the supremacy of the Civil Service by crushing any class that should rise in stature to it, and that it is the duty of a Government to make the bargains between its subjects. Hence these proclamations, these encouragements, to the Ryots not to sow—for it would be mere prevarication, when you had told a prepaid hoveller that he need not sow, to aver that you did not exhort him not to sow— and hence those memorable interferences with the course of British justice.

How could concessions be made in the face of such acts as these?   There was the Lieut.-Governor, leading in a new Saturnian Age, coming to the rescue.   How could the planter expect the Ryot to listen to easy methods of working out advances, when Mr. Grant and Mr. Eden told him he need not work at all—for to sow means to work, so far as the planter is concerned—and where every concession made would only be thought a sacrifice to palliate the ire of Mr. Grant?

When he had done this, Mr. Grant looked on complacently, and wrote home to say—He knew it must come.   If he had told the Home Government the truth, he would have said—He was determined to do it.   He did it wilfully, and by the boldest means. He, never having any right to interfere in any way in the matter, now taunts us with not having made concessions, when he interrupted us in the process, and rendered them impossible.

Even he himself is now driven to promise some concessions to his wretched salt Ryots, but they are not yet made. Those people are now literally starving. Suppose we had sent emissaries among them. It would have been easy to raise those poor hungry creatures, languishing in their forced labour. But Mr. Grant has only to decide, and he still deliberates : we had free men to deal with, and we had to bargain. But he takes his time while these men starve, and he rushes down to crush us because we were in a momentary difficulty, and it was a chance to ruin an independent class of Englishmen.

This is the reply which we make to Mr. Temple when he exhorts us to make concessions, and to advance our offers with the increase of prices of food and labour. We are not, and never have been, such fools as not to know that this must be done. Mr. Temple must not measure the knowledge of commercial men in such matters by the state of thick darkness which he and Mr. Fergusson found at the Board of the Indigo Commission; or by the state of mind of that eminent official, who writes minutes on capital and labour which would astonish Adam Smith, and who thinks it the duty of a Government to fix, with popular proclamations, and with a phantasmagoria of ever-changing magistrates, the price of indigo leaves. But we must make these advances and these concessions in our own way, and in our Ryots' way, as we can afford, and as they will find them advantageous. We cannot nail an indigo broker by the ears till he buys our indigo in the Manchester market at a stated price, nor an indigo Ryot by the ears till he has brought us his twenty bundles per beegah in the Mofussil. The hazards of the indigo manufacturer are very great; even as great as the manufacture is beneficial to the country and the people of India. No capitalist runs these hazards, without the hope of his profits being larger than if his money were embarked in what is considered a perfectly secure investment. But, looking to the past, there have been but few fortunes made by indigo, and the balances on the books of the great houses that failed between 1830 and 1832, and again in 1847, tell a very different tale to there having been any thing like inordinate profits among the indigo planters. With reduced expenditure and a greater economy, of late years, the concerns in those districts where they have had favourable weather, have been doing well. In other districts the planter has had to contend with the usual dangers—too much or too little rain; too much or too little sun; storms, caterpillars, locusts, and white ants; and, finally, the greatest white ant of all, the Government, personified in Mr. J. P. Grant.

Yet the Government cannot complain that the planters were not ductile and humble. When it appeared certain that Mr. J. P. Grant would not allow the planters to conduct their own business; when Mr. Grant had practically outlawed them, and had shut the labour-market against them, and had appointed a commission to ascertain upon what terms they should be allowed to trade;

when the commission had split into two sections, and the
majority had been delivered of a Report, which, for partiality, ignorance, and absurdity, is the pattern State-
paper of India, deserving only to be docketted with Mr.
Grant's Minute, Mr. Eden's perwannahs, and Mr. Herschel's pattern decision : when all this had been accomplished, and the indigo lands lay all unsown, and the factories closed, the planters recognised the position which
Mr. Grant had assumed as the despotic licenser of trade,
and wrote him a proposal, under which they hoped that
this Government trades-union would stop the strike, and
allow the eight millions of dead capital to operate, and
the two millions of trade returns annually to circulate in
the Mofussil.   Here is the letter—

" TO THE SECRETARY TO THE GOVERNMENT OF BENGAL.

" SIR,—I am directed by the Central Committee of the
Indigo Planters' Association to submit to you, for the
information of His Honour the Lieutenant-Governor of
Bengal, the following suggestions as to changes in the
system of Ryottee indigo cultivation which the Committee have, as regards planters, recommended for general
adoption in Lower Bengal.

" That the contract be in the simplest form practicable,
signed by both parties stipulating in the case of the
Ryottee cultivation, on the one side for the cultivation of
a certain quantity of land, and on the other side, for payment of the plant at a certain price.

" Contracts for labour, carts, boats, &c. &c., to be in
similar simple forms.

" That on signing the contract an advance be made in

cash of a certain sum per beegah, out of which say eight annas per beegah shall be a separate and specific payment for the use and occupation of the land; the size of the beegah to be specified in the contract.

" That the factory shall bear all the expense of providing seed, stamps, and carriage, for which the planter shall pay separately, leaving to the Ryot only the ploughing, sowing, weeding, and cutting.

" That the planter shall pay to the Ryot for the plant a price to be specified in the contract, and which the Committee believe, will, for the ensuing season, in almost all cases, except chur lands, be at the rate of four bundles per rupee in Lower Bengal.

" That should the number of bundles realized from the beegah be insufficient to cover the advance made, then the loss shall be borne equally by the planter and the Ryot.

" That all accounts with the Ryots shall be settled annually, as soon as practicable after the close of the manufacture, and that whatever fazil, or balance may be due to the Ryot shall be paid to him in cash.

" That in the event of the Ryot artfully or fraudulently evading the contract fairly entered into, or neglecting the cultivation, he shall be punishable, as provided by Act XI. of 1860, or as provided by Sections 2 and 3 of Act V. of 1830, or by a penalty of five times the amount advanced to be summarily recovered.

" I have to remark, in the first place, that the price to be paid for the bundle of plant must be left for individual adjustment. One rule and one price could not hold good, or be fair in the case of plant, the produce of the churs of the rivers, cultivated with little or no trouble, and scarcely requiring weeding, and in the case of plant grown on rich and heavy high lands; but it is evident that a fair price, remunerating to the Ryot, must be given, or he will not undertake the cultivation.   .

"Secondly—To clause 5 it will, no doubt, be objected, that the new system still involves the chance of balance accumulating against the Ryot.   The Committee will regret much if this should be the result, but they feel that, unless some responsibility attaches to the Ryot, he will not perform his engagement or cultivate properly.

" If the Ryot was certain of enjoying his advance without interest, whether there be a crop or not, the planters think the consequences will be that there will be no crop.

" In the manufacture of salt, in the cultivation of opium, and of all other crops, the risk remains with the Ryots ; but in consideration of the precarious nature of the indigo crop in Lower Bengal, the Committee recommends that only half the risk, as regards liability for cash advanced for cultivation, should be borne by the Ryot.

" The Committee trust that, in the case of contracts fairly and freely entered into on these or similar terms, the indigo planters will have the protection of a law similar to Act XI. of 1860, or to the rescinded clauses of Act V. of 1830, so that they may not suffer ruinous loss from the violation of engagements as to indigo plant, which would certainly be the case if they were referred to a Civil suit for redress.

" I have the honour to be, Sir,

" Your most obedient servant,

(Signed)   " W. F. FERGUSSON,

" *Secretary.*"

In this position Mr. Grant has gained his point. Whether he accept or refuse the tender of the Planters' Association, he has succeeded in subjugating the whole class to the Civil Service, even to the making them take from the Civil Service the prices at which they shall deal, and the terms on which they shall buy produce. He has reduced it now to this, that independent British commerce must dwindle away, or the Civil Service of India must be reduced to a level with other classes of gentlemen in India. As it now exists the Civil Service is an anachronism; it is hostile to all the principles of free commerce; it is tyrannical; a meddler with the course of justice and with the private dealings of men; a despot doing despotism upon old-world fancies of regulating prices and keeping up exclusive castes. Either that foolish Service, which will not learn, must go; or British capital must fly, and India must go back to what it was in the time of Lord Cornwallis, when, as that Governor-General declared, one-third of the Company's territories were jungle.

CHAPTER XII.

CONCLUSION.

IT is not a satisfactory success to have proved that we are sinking to ruin. Nor is it great reason for joy to have shewn that this position has been, as we believe, wantonly brought about by a man who seems to combine in himself every mischievous quality which a man in power can have, and yet who still is in power.

We have had to develop in these pages the ancient traditionary policy of the East India Company and its servants to keep all independent British capitalists out of India ; and, when they could no longer keep them out, to discourage them as much as possible. We have had to tell how, when they struggled in, bringing blessings with them, the Civil Service have uniformly used the power which every despotic Government has over an Asiatic people, to make these British settlers not only landless outlaws, but outlaws whom the natives were excited to defraud. We have been obliged also to recount how, when in early times they raised their hand to defend those interests which the law left undefended, they were misrepresented and calumniated in England as desperadoes and lawless ruffians.

We have, further, had to trace how, when by their energy and perseverance, and by aid of the sympathy of

their countrymen at home, they emerged, to a partial degree, from this state of outlawry, and created little circles
of civilization around them, they were still pursued by
constant calumnies, and were always being made the objects of accusations, which successive Governors-General
have carefully investigated, and have uniformly dismissed
as groundless

We have proved, also, from a concurrence of the most
opposite testimony, that the planters, as a body, have always been kind in their treatment and faithful in their
dealings with the natives; that they have made the barren
wilderness to smile ; that they have made the season of
famine tolerable ; that they have been the only refuge to
the small cultivators in their frequent moments of distress; that they have been money-lenders without interest, physicians without recompence, arbitrators without
fees, forbearing landlords, and indulgent creditors. We
have proved these facts by the unwilling admissions of
magistrates, judges, collectors, and Zemindars ; and have
sealed their authenticity by the authority of the greatest
statesmen whom India has ever received at the hands of
England. We have explained that all this has so happened, not because Indigo manufacturers are better than
other Englishmen, but because they have seen their true
interest in working their way by kindness ; and have been
compelled, by the conditions of their isolated position
among an improvident, necessitous, and ignorant multitude, to exercise to their advantage their superior provi-
dence, and their better knowledge of the charities of life,
and the resources of science. We have shewn that the
natural and the actual result has been, that where indigo

is cultivated the Ryot is better fed, better clothed, and better cared for than where indigo is unknown; and we have called forth those two natives, who are almost the only natives known to the Western world at once for their wealth, their charity, their patriotism, and their philosophy, who have proclaimed it as the result of all their life-long experience that these British settlers have done more to benefit India and the Hindoo than any other class of men, whether in or out of the Service.

Against this picture we have been obliged to set that of the persecutors, who at Calcutta have had the power of making laws, and who have always seen in this independent class of country gentlemen enemies to the monopolies which they cherished, the abuses which they desired to hide, and the supremacy which they very naturally valued. We have shewn that when the British settlers made known to the people of England the character of the Company's dealings with the princes of India, the Company retaliated with fabled accusations against the planters in the Mofussil; that when the British settlers exposed the national losses sustained by the Company's commercial monopolies, the Company retaliated by refusing to allow the planters to hold land; that when the planters persuaded their countrymen against renewing the Company's charter, the Company's *officers retaliated by withdrawing the remedies which they had in* 1830 *enjoyed by the law for the enforcement of their indigo contracts*—and which they re-enacted with more stringent clauses for their own protection against the opium Ryots a few years afterwards; and that when the British settlers attempted to shew the English public how much the evil organization of the Civil Service had to do with the mutinies, the Civil Service once more retorted by obtaining the withdrawal of that power of calling up their tenants and cultivators to attend their audits, which all Zemindars, both British and native, had previously enjoyed.

We have shewn, also, how one step further down had placed the two classes in still stronger antagonism; how the British settlers made known in England the great evil of the old Indian cozenage; and how they pressed upon public opinion at home the propriety of breaking up the " Nobility of India," and opening it to the competition of the whole youth of Britain and Ireland. We have quoted the evidence that has been given before Committees; and we have confessed in the production of that evidence, which was but a small part of what was really done, abundant provocation to arouse the anger of the remnant of the old unreformed Civil Service.

Lastly, we have narrated by what arts the present representative in Bengal of that Service has avenged his caste and himself. That he should hate us, we do not wonder; that he should ruin us, if he could lawfully, perhaps we have no great right to complain. He has been nurtured in traditions which are the direct contradictories of the policy of the British Parliament and of the interests of the British people. It is his to keep India for the Civil Service, as his predecessors have in former days done: it is our interest and your interest, and it is the declared desire of Parliament, to open India to all colours and to all classes. We and you, and Mr. J. P. Grant, cannot but be enemies; and Mr. Grant cannot but see evil in all you do and in all we achieve. We have never reproached him with his hostility.

The accusation which we have made, and in support of which we have offered, as we submit, proof enough to urge you to inquiry, is not that he has struck at us, but that he has struck us foully. We say that he has used his official power unfairly to our destruction. We say that he has used the influence intrusted to him, in order to preserve peace and goodwill among all classes in Bengal, to the end of arousing the populace against our houses, our property, and our trade. We say that he has abused a mere administrative power, intrusted to him for routine purposes, to the end of influencing the decisions of judicial officers and violating the independence of judicial action. We say that he has arrested industry, banished capital, shut up trade, aroused evil passions, excited the populace, and threatened the magistrates; and that he has assumed, to evil ends, an absolute dominion alike over the commercial dealings of his subjects and over the decisions of their disputes.

All this we have proved with, at least, sufficient certainty to justify his suspension from functions which he has so perilously abused. We are not execrating, we are impeaching. We are not pelting a man with epithets, we are building up round him a prison of facts. If he shall be able, before a fairly-named Committee of the House of Commons, or such other court of inquiry as the country may approve, to shew that he was justified in destroying our commerce and violating our right to justice, we shall have nothing left but to succumb; and shall have only the miserable satisfaction of knowing that

England is prepared to lose ten millions of capital and two annual millions of trade, rather than set the precedent of dismissing a man who has played the tyrant madly in a high office.

But this will not be all. It is ours to-day, for ours is the only large independent interest in India; but it will be the silk manufacturer's to-morrow; it will be the tea manufacturer's should he grow to be a rival; it will be the cotton and the flax growers if they cannot be shut out by lack of roads and if railways should eventually give them a possibility of holding their own.* Against such men as Governor Grant and the myrmidons whom he has at his back, and against the unscrupulous manner in which he uses his power, no industry can stand,† and no capital can live.

---

* The cotton grower, the flax grower, and the indigo grower are one in interest in India. By advances all must work; and all must be at the mercy of any Governor who may choose to dislike their system or find fault with their prices, or hate themselves, and who may work out his will by informing the prepaid cultivator that Government does not desire them to fulfil their contracts.

† Read how this Lieut.-Governor is still, at this moment, going on. We take this story from a recent letter from the Calcutta correspondent of *The Times:*—

"The special Act passed six months ago for the speedy settlement of disputes between the planter and the Ryot has expired, and the former is now literally at the mercy of the latter. The cultivators of the soil, encouraged by their past victory, by the declared inaction of Government, and by the prospect, too, of being able to avoid the payment of rent, have refused very generally either to take advances or to perform their contracts; in some cases they have even sown the planter's own land with their own seed, and, although not proceeding to actual violence, they have placed an embargo on supplies of fowls, ducks, and other necessaries of life which the planters were in the habit of receiving from the villages, and have even in some districts compelled their native servants to leave them. The attitude of the planters has been, meanwhile, in the highest degree praiseworthy; they have been guilty of no infraction of the law; they have witnessed their lands ploughed up and their supplies of fresh provisions cut off without a murmur;

Than our present position nothing can be worse.   Our
factories are closed.   We ourselves are, some of us, with
a whimsical parody of justice, bound over to keep the
peace, because the Ryots, instigated by Mr. Grant's proclamations, are threatening to attack our houses.   Men

they see ruin staring them in the face, and they can do no more than
sit in their factories and be still.   Their property is gradually melting
before their eyes, and, hard-headed, hard-working moneyed men as they
are, they are forced to submit.   It is in vain that they have appealed
for redress.   The Government of India and the Government of Bengal
have both decided that matters must be left as they are.   In spite of
advice to the contrary from the planters, who are of opinion that Mr.
Grant's proclamations are always misunderstood by the Ryots, a proclamation to this effect has been issued.   It purports, indeed, to warn
the Ryots, that unless they perform their contracts they will render
themselves liable to civil suits in the Civil Courts.   To those who are
acquainted with the delay and expense attendant upon these suits the
warning seems little more than a mockery.   In that light the Ryots
have regarded it; they have not sown, and they have refused to perform
their contracts.   The case of the indigo planters was never so desperate
as now; and when it is considered that all they demand is the establishment of district courts, with summary powers, to prevent the Ryots
evading their obligations, and the absence of interference on the part of
the Lieutenant-Governor of Bengal, it would seem that to leave them
entirely unprotected is to sacrifice them designedly.

" Whatever may be the intentions or secret wishes of the Lieutenant-
Governor of Bengal with respect to the planters, and to non-official
Europeans generally, the measures he carries out are not calculated to
impress them with an idea that he is in favour of their settlement in the
country.   With respect to this question of indigo, *the civil officer who so
ably administered the affairs of the Jessore district* (Mr. E. W. Molony)
*received certainly no reward for his zeal.   The gentleman, on the con-
trary, who originally fomented the disturbances, and the civil officer who
mismanaged everything in Kishnagur, have been promoted over the heads
of several seniors.*   Again, within the last few days a gentleman—Mr.
Spooner—has arrived for the purpose of representing the Presidencies
of Madras and Bombay in a Committee set on foot by the late Mr.
Wilson, and the object of which is the examination and possible revision
of the *ad valorem* duties on imports.   To form the Committee the
Chamber of Commerce appointed its President, Mr. Bullen; *and the
Lieutenant-Governor, in his turn, appointed Mr. Eden, a young civilian, known for his unrelenting hostility to the mercantile community,*
to be the third member of a Committee in which the interests of that
community were so largely concerned."

whose whole stock of ploughs and bullocks are bought with our money, laugh us to scorn if we ask them to sow indigo for us in liquidation of some portion of the free loans they are now enjoying. Meanwhile, Mr. Grant appoints Mr. Eden to place after place of honour and profit, just as old tyrants piled honours on their favourites to insult their people ; and that no doubt may exist as to his intentions, he exalts the boys, whose decisions please him, over the heads of their seniors, and passes over with marked neglect the sober men who were not zealous enough to light the flame of social war through the districts where his enemies dwelt.

Surely this is a case for the interference of the British people and the British Parliament. Our prayer is not for money, or for soldiers, or for protective duties. We ask only for that protection of law which you yourselves enjoy, and which it is the first duty of Government to give. We ask not to be helped, but to be let alone, even as you are let alone in your business affairs. We ask to be relieved from the oppression of an ignorant and mischievous despot, who is ruining the finest country of the earth, who is even now rendering it necessary to take military occupation of the rural districts of Bengal, and who, if he remain your Minister, will soon bring matters to such a pass that you will have to make your choice between abandoning the country and holding it at the point of the bayonet.

APPENDIX.

I.—Extracts of Letters from Merchants, Planters, and others, in Bengal, respecting the present condition of the Indigo Trade and Manufacture.

II.—Extracts from the Honourable Ashley Eden's Evidence before the Indigo Committee, 1860.

III.—The Petition of the Indigo Planters Association to Lord Canning against Mr. Grant.

IV.—Reply of the Indigo Planters Association to Mr. Grant.

V.—Latest accounts contained in the Calcutta Newspapers.

APPENDICES.

I.

EXTRACTS OF LETTERS FROM MERCHANTS AND INDIGO MANU-
FACTURERS IN BENGAL, RESPECTING THE PRESENT CONDITION
OF THE INDIGO TRADE AND MANUFACTURE.

From MESSRS. JARDINE, SKINNER, *and* Co., *of Calcutta.*

Dated Calcutta, 8th October, 1860.

WE regret to have to report more unfavourably than ever
of the state of our northern Indigo concerns. The Ryots are
becoming daily more bold and defiant, and openly assert their
determination to put a stop to the cultivation both Ryotty and
Neiz. They have latterly and very generally taken possession
of our Neiz Jhote lands—some of which we hold on sub-lease
from themselves, and some direct from Government and Zemindars—and have sown them down with their own crops. We
are referred for redress to Act 4 of 1840, under which a
magistrate is authorized to keep in possession the party he may
find to be in possession at the time of investigation; in some
instances the magistrates have decreed the lands to us; but in
others, they refuse to decide on the rights of the matter in
dispute, and refer us to the Civil Courts. Our assistants are
refused supplies; our head native servants threatened and
insulted to such an extent that many have resigned, and our
ploughmen and coolies so intimidated, that they refuse to work
any longer for us. Large bodies of men on two occasions
surrounded two of the factories during the night, but retired
after making a great noise on seeing our people prepared for
them; under such circumstances, we see no hope of any
October sowings on the part of the Ryots, nor can we look
for any in spring either, unless the Government, either
here or at home, take prompt and energetic measures to break
up the present illegal combination. Of Neiz sowings even,
we must fall very much short of what we would, under other
circumstances, have got in, and there is, moreover, danger of
the Ryots breaking up our lands so sown, and sowing them
down with their own crops. We wholly and entirely attribute

the present state of affairs to the course pursued by the Bengal Government. The Ryots are firmly convinced that it is the wish of Government that Indigo cultivation should be put a stop to, and that they will be supported in their illegal proceedings so long as they do not proceed to open violence. Where a Ryot alleges trespass against a Planter, the magistrates are enjoined to support the Ryot; but where a Planter brings a like charge against a Ryot, he, in his turn, is referred to the Civil Court. In our own case, all our Ryots are under contract for a term of five years, of which, with the great majority, three and four have still to run; and yet the Lieutenant-Governor, in a proclamation issued some months ago, distinctly told all Ryots connected with Indigo, that after this year (30th September last) they would be at liberty to sow and take advances or not, as they chose. Until this notification became known, all our concerns were quite quiet, and work progressing as usual; but since then, they have gradually become disorganized, till, at the present moment, they are in as bad a state as any of those in Kishnughur and Jessore. It is now known that Government will not enact any special law of contract, or take any action on the report of the Indigo Commissioners, except by introducing small Cause Courts into the Mofussil; but as they propose establishing them for the present only in the large towns, they will practically be of no service in the present crisis. We have addressed Government several times, pointing out the hardships we are suffering under; but as yet have got no redress. We intend to send you copies of these papers by an early opportunity, and would impress on you that unless measures of relief are devised by the Home Government, and the Bengal Government be strictly enjoined to carry them out fully and speedily, the cultivation of Indigo must, in a very great measure, cease,—entailing ruin to many, and serious loss and depreciation of property to all, planters.

From MESSRS. JARDINE, SKINNER, *and* Co., *of Calcutta.*

Dated 8th November, 1860.

WE regret that we cannot report any improvement in the state of things.

There is not yet any improvement in the Indigo districts, and even where partial sowings have been made, a great proportion will be destroyed by cattle, or will fail in consequence of inefficient cultivation and want of weeding, defects which, in the absence of labour, it is impossible to supply.

23rd November, 1860.

Little or no further progress has been made in the sowings; in fact, it is now too late in the season to continue them. In the Bansbarreah quarter, where the Ryots have hitherto kept pretty quiet, they have suddenly become very bold and turbulent, instigated, we believe, by two Zemindars. The Gomastah was attacked in open day close to the factory, and severely maltreated. The magistrate and military police were speedily on the spot.

Had the authorities generally shewn equal promptitude at an earlier period, we would not now have to regret the state of anarchy to which the Indigo districts have been brought. The Zemindars were also summoned to appear, but, we hear, have absconded from the district. Since then two of our factory bungalows have been burned down. Government has offered a reward of 1,000 rupees for discovery of the incendiaries, but as yet without success.

3rd December, 1860.

The incendiaries who burned down our two bungalows have not yet been discovered. ———

From EDWARD PRESTWICH, *Esq., a Merchant in Calcutta, and Joint Proprietor in some of the most extensive Indigo Properties in Bengal, dated Calcutta, 23rd November,* 1860.

I AM sorry I am unable to report any improvement in Indigo prospects. My tour this year was to the following places, Burdwan, Rajmahal, Jungypore, Calleegunge, Banleah, Ackrigunge, Berhampore, Patkabarree, Khalbolia, and also Neeschindipore. The opinion of the leading planters appears to be that the present movement is not simply one of the Indigo Ryot against the planter, but of the native against the European, and this view is confirmed by the fact that the combination is not confined to Ryots who have contracted to sow Indigo, but includes the natives generally, the head men of the villages being the leaders. I will describe to you the state of the Patkabarree concern. The Ryots there have never complained until the present year. There are, in round numbers, 7,000 Biggahs Neezabad, and 8,000 Biggahs Ryottee, with 2,200 Ryots who sow Indigo. This year, half that number cleared off their balances, and have rupees 10,000 to receive from the factory as fazil. The rent they have to pay is from 10 annas to 1 rupee per biggah. They sow two crops upon the ground, at one and the same time, so that one cultivation does for the two crops and no weeding is required; both crops are sown in October; one crop say of wheat, oats, hay, or the like, matures first in the spring, and is then garnered in. The Indigo then shoots a-head, and in its turn is cut and manufactured. Conjointly these are the best and most profitable crops to the Ryot that he can sow. *This year, not one Ryot will sow Indigo, and the whole of our own Neezabad land consisting of 7,000 Beegahs has, with a few exceptions, been taken possession of by the Ryots, and sown down in Kullye.* Our servants are intimidated by the Ryots, and leave us. Our lands we may recover under Act IV, but our October sowings are lost. The season for sowing is past, and we must take our chance in the spring.* When I was there, I required bearers to carry me on in my palkee. I sent for them and their reply was, that had I been a respectable native they would carry me willingly; but being a belatee sahib (or English gentleman) they would see me far enough. Shortly before my arrival, *the out-buildings were fired during the night and some were burned down. The manager was aroused from his bed; he could get no assistance from the neighbouring villagers, who are, indeed, upon good grounds, supposed to be the incendiaries,* and had not the wind lulled, our seed golahs, full of seed, and the factory houses would also have gone. As it was, flakes of fire fell on the cutcha roofs of the former, and the cutcha verandah of the latter, and they were with difficulty extinguished. The next morning, a messenger with a note was dispatched by the manager to the magistrate. The villagers, guessing his errand, knocked the messenger off his horse; but the police, fearful for themselves, rescued him. A counter-charge, however, of the murder of two of the police who are both alive and well, has been brought against him. These men were present before the magistrate when the charge was made, and were seen by him. Our man has, nevertheless, been bound down to appear when called for, in a sum of rupees 500; but whether to answer the charge of murder, or to prosecute for the assault, I do not know. One of the assistants of the concern has been twice assaulted this year, once severely. He identified his assailants upon oath before the magistrate; but they were discharged because he could get no witnesses. No witnesses are procurable. The willing, if there are any such, are afraid to appear, and the unwilling won't. The assistant, appeared to think that his life was not safe, or that the risk of such assaults was not included in his salary of rupees 200 per month, or that he ought to have received some protection from the magistrate, and the offenders punished. At all events, he did not like it,

---

* Kullye being a crop, not requiring cultivation, lands sown with it, become as hard as iron, and on them a spring crop of Indigo cannot be grown.

and sent in his resignation. I may add, that he was riding alone along the road, when the assault was committed. These things I heard from the manager, and have no reason to doubt his words.

It is on the subject of rents that the managers are so uneasy: they say, that they believe the combination will extend, as it is now extending, to a refusal to pay rents, and when it comes to that, it will be utterly useless for the planter to contend against it. In such a case, to 'attempt to collect our rents through the Courts would be utterly impracticable, and for Government then to refer us to our legal remedy would be simply another insult and mockery, added to the many they have already heaped upon us. With a Government supposed, and a police known, to be against the individual planter, surrounded as he is by hundreds of thousands of hostile, non-paying Ryots, with magistrates luke-warm in our favour, to say the least of it, and insufficient even now for a tithe of the work they have to do, what will be the result when their work becomes ten thousand fold? When, however, things come to that pass, Government will be at a dead lock, and will have to do something in self defence. What the planter requires from Government is not much. *He says, that the whole of the people and the police believe that the Government is against us;* and in this opinion he is confirmed by almost all of the best and most intelligent persons with whom I have spoken on the subject. If the Government will cause the people and the police to understand that such is not the case, the aspect of affairs would be changed in a day. Let Mr. Grant instruct the magistrates and officials simply to explain this clearly and intelligibly (and it would be very easy to do this), and our difficulties would be at an end.

From an extensive Planter in Kishnaghur.

Dated 4th November, 1860.

GOVERNMENT has steadily persevered in the determination to root us all out of the Mofussil. Many thought that Mr. Grant's malice would have been gorged with the total ruin of our Indigo interests; he has also ruined our Zemindarree. The Ryots finding they got every support in sowing down our Neezabad with "kullye," refused to pay rents, and many Putnees have not collected a pice for 1267 (A.D. 1860—1861). Our instalments with the Zemindars are payable monthly; we have had to pay up as usual, and must do so as long as we have a rag to our backs. I have tried to recover through Court. I com-

M

plained in January, got a decree on 28th May, and the case is
now under appeal, and likely to stick there until next January.
In another instance, after six months I got a decree for rents.
The officers of the Court went with my Gomastah to attach the
property; the Ryots turned out, and nearly killed a couple of
the Court people, and severely maltreated the others. After
another four months' litigation the Ryots were sentenced to
four months' imprisonment, and I am as near getting my rents
as I was a year ago. These two instances are in properties in
which we have no Indigo. Mr. Grant now tells me to go to
Court if the Ryots refuse to pay rents. After the above
experience am I likely to do so? There is no course left us but
to sell the Putnees for what they will fetch, and wash our hands of
all landed interest in the country. We cannot go on paying
rents if we cannot collect them; and the Government will take
good care we never get any law that will enable us to get in
our rents monthly, as we have to pay them. With the present
feelings of the Ryots, no terms will induce them to sow Indigo.
Unless you were on the spot, you could never believe that a
people could be so changed in one short year. It has become
altogether a matter of race. The Ryots are just as bitter
against the officers of the railway as against the planter. The
Brahmins keep up the excitement, and have been the leaders on
all occasions. They really believe we must all leave India.
The combination is general, and effectually carried out,—the
policy being passive resistance. The Salgurmoodiah concern has
stopped *all* Indigo cultivation; and, indeed, it is folly to have
sowings, for the Ryots will destroy the crop with cattle. Not a
witness, nor, in fact, a servant, can be had, and every officer of
Government looks upon it as much as his appointment is worth
to give an order in favour of a planter. There will be no
October crop, for the few concerns that may sow a portion will
be as bad as the rest before March. I see no prospect of
coming to an arrangement with the Ryots. It is impossible
that the withdrawal of 7 lakhs of rupees (70,000*l.*) from our
concerns in one year can be done without affecting the country
generally. I am merely carrying on the Copannee to keep the
Boonahs (private labourers) together, and doing my best to get
in the rents quietly. The disaffection has extended to Purneah,
where, I hear, Forbes's Ryots refuse to sow. Tirhoot and
Behar, inclusive of the opium, will be the next move, and as
the income tax has not yet come into operation, the Government cannot realize the extent of their difficulties. They have
stood hitherto like the Missionaries—men who gave, and asked
for no return. They have now to acquire a knowledge of

Bengalee character by asking for payment of a tax, without ever having given an advance, and in the mean time they have destroyed the entire European influence and interest which would have been a back stay in their hour of need. Every rupee I had earned I have in these properties. I felt confident that, with our great landed interest and the liberal manner in which these concerns were carried on, nothing but prosperity could attend us. Who could ever have foreseen that the Government would set to work, in the most inveterate manner, to destroy all our capital, and drive us, after years of toil, to leave the district? With every Ryot's heart turned against us, what can we do? How is it possible to escape loss, and, if we hang on, total ruin? It might be a different matter if we had to deal with 50 or 100 tenants; and people at home argue as if our business were confined to a small estate, instead of thinking how helpless a man must become with not only the 23,000 Ryots, with whom he has engagements turning upon him, but when the millions who surround him detest him because he has a white skin. It is our enormous extent of country and dealings, which people who have never been in India cannot grasp.

I only trust all will join heart and soul to try and save us something out of the wreck. If Mr. J. P. Grant is allowed to remain in power, we are without hope.

I have given you a long letter, and wish I could have given you better news.

***

From the same Planter. .

Dated 6th December, 1860.

THE Ryots find the combination answers admirably. They are all now in clover, paying no rents, and having the knowledge that through the Civil Court we can no more recover rents from thousands of people than we can recover our Indigo balances. We are virtually without redress. We are now as helpless as to rents as we were as to Indigo. The Ryots refer us to the Court. You thought Government would interfere and save us: but no,—we, as Putneedars, must first be driven out. The Zemindars will then have to collect directly from the Ryots, and unless they can do so without difficulty, the Government rents will remain unpaid. *Then,* but not *till then,* will the Government support the landholder, and by that time we shall have disappeared. Experience tells too truly also that rents once in arrear can never be recovered from the Ryot; he is the most improvident being on the face of the earth; and like all men of the East, he invariably lives beyond his income, and is never clear of the Mahajun's books. These latter worthies are now reaping the fruits of their instigating the Ryots not to sow Indigo, and the Moonsiff's courts are completely glutted with plaints. Owing to the threats of the combination ringleaders in this immediate neighbourhood, many of our Tuhsildars (rent collectors) have not returned since the Poojah (native holidays), and I find it impossible to replace them, no man consenting to become an outcaste for the sake of employment. The non-payment of rents is not a criminal offence, and the instigators cannot, therefore, be touched. I hear that the railway engineers have represented to Government that they find there is a complete combination against the *European;* no amount of pay will induce the Joyrampoor fellows to work on the line, and where men have been brought from Santipoor (thirty miles off,) to make bricks, these Joyrampoor scoundrels have intimidated the strangers, who are daily running away. The unfortunate contractors are in the position we were during the manufacturing. The work must be done, and these fellows can make their own terms. As it is, the contractors are just paying 150 to 200 per cent. above what is fair and right; not owing to competition, but to the unfortunate state of the country, which is without a Government,— which knows not law or justice. The Brahmins look upon *us* as the despised of the Company Bahadoor, and we are bullied by great and small. The income tax appears to halt, which is a pity. The Government will discover the character of the people when they come to seek something from them; the passive resistance so ably carried out regarding rents will completely floor Government at every step. You will see by R. Thomas and Co.'s Circular, of 3rd December, a very truthful representation of the writer's, and, in fact, every one's, difficulties. The Ryots who are well disposed towards us have no support or protection, and are ruined and disgraced as is therein described.

From MESSRS. THOMAS *and* Co's., *Price Current and Indigo Report, printed in the Calcutta Correspondence of " The Times," of 7th January,* 1861.

OUR market having opened we beg to hand you particulars of the transactions that have already taken place. Only one public sale has been held as yet, at which prices ranged for the fine lots from July rates to 2*d.* advance, and for the middling and common sorts July rates to 2*d.* discount.

Private Sales.—W. G. and Co., Pundoul, Tirhoot, 2,000 maunds, at 187r. 8a.; Moran, Mooteearree, &c., Tirhoot 1,500 maunds, at 197r. 8a.; Moran, Mooteearree, &c., Tirhoot, 300 maunds, at 200r.; K. E. J. W., Bansbareah, Kishnaghur, 83 chests, at 202r. 8a.

Public Sales.—A. and J. L., Rampoorah, Moorshedabad, 20 chests, at 198r. 10a.; H. and Co., L., Loknathpore, Kishnaghur, 21 chests, at 200r. 1a.; H. and Co., L. B., Khalispore, Kishnaghur, 42 chests, at 170r. 7a.; I. C., J. E., Connoynutsal, Burdwan, 25 chests, at 162r.; H. S. and Co., B., Beezoolce, Jessore, 50 chests, at 205r. 6a.; H. S. and Co., G., Goldar, Jessore, 11 chests at 206r. 13a.; J., H. M., J., Jingurgatcha, Jessore, 21 chests, at 212r. 15a.

In our circular of the 8th of September we alluded to the delay in giving the report of the Indigo Commission to the public; a similar delay has now taken place on the part of the Lieutenant-Governor of Bengal in making his report upon it known to the public. The document has now been in his Honour's hands for three months, and when it is remembered how urgently he pressed on the sitting of the Commission, and hurried the members of it for their report, we think that those concerned in the great interest in jeopardy have further just ground of complaint against Mr. Grant, for this neglect of the report.

The extension of the conspiracy and combination against Indigo cultivation in the Furreedpore District has been marked by events in one concern of which we give the narrative, as well illustrating the position in which planters are placed. In the Cossimpore concern the whole sowings, cultivation and manufacture of the past season were completed without any sign of objection on the part of the Ryots; when the work was over they all came to the factory as usual, settled their accounts, expressed themselves as perfectly contented, and gladly took advances for the new season, signing agreements on stamp paper in the most stringent form, rendering themselves liable to penalties of 10 rupees per Beegah for non-fulfilment of their contracts. At first the ploughing and sowing went on as usual, and all was perfectly quiet in the concern; but suddenly without any apparent cause, the Ryots all discontinued the cultivation, and went to the magistrate in the usual way with petitions against the factory. This official acted with the greatest fairness and consideration, pointed out to the people that the fact of their having taken advances and signed contracts was of too recent date and too fully capable of proof for denial, and that if they persisted in refusing to sow, decrees must be given against them, and ruin overtake them. He also read to them the Proclamation, stating that it was not true that Government wished the cultivation of indigo to cease. All, however, proved of no avail; the people were evidently under some evil influence, and only replied they had been told that they must petition against sowing Indigo.

Mr. Grant has remarked, as mentioned by us in our circular of the 8th of October, that the capacity for organization and combined action shown by the people is a subject worthy of much consideration; surely, also, the fact of some evil influence being at work, sufficiently powerful to over-ride that of the Government, as expressed by the Proclamation, deserves the most serious consideration, and the most strenuous exertions of the Government to suppress. We can confidently assert that twelve months ago no such antagonistic power existed, and that the word of a magistrate would have been implicitly accepted by the people on any subject even without the support of a Proclamation of Government. The moral influence exercised by the authorities over the people is entirely broken down, and it has become their regular custom, whenever cases are given against them by the magistrates, in favour of Indigo Planters, to come to Calcutta with petitions to the Lieutenant-Governor, whom they state to be their friend, and certain to reverse the decisions unfavourable to them.

We feel that it must be so difficult for people in England to realize to themselves the position into which property has been brought in Lower Bengal by Mr. Grant's system of Government that we annex to this the copy of a letter from one of our largest planters and most valued constituents, for the absolute truth of every word in which, we give our fullest assurance. The writer of the letter, we beg it to be understood, is in precisely the same relative position as any gentleman residing in the midst of his own landed property in England, and there is nothing whatever in the tenure of his estates, or his claims upon his tenantry for rent, to which such a state of things as he describes can be attributed; the same might as easily occur in Yorkshire did the same absence of effective laws exist there as in Bengal, and the same determination on the part of Government not to protect the landowner against the encroachments of his tenantry.

The refusal of the Ryots to pay rents to planters continues as general and determined as ever. In some parts of the country, deputy collectors have been sent into many villages to decide cases under Act X on the spot, as without the adoption of this plan the work of the Courts would be simply impossible.

The recovery of their *neej* lands by the planters under Act IV is slowly progressing, but in many instances decrees are of of little use, as the authorities will not give sufficient force of police to carry them out when the Ryots resist the ordinary establishments, which they have frequently done; and in nearly every case the recovery of these lands has been too late in the season, and when the Kulai crops sown by the Ryots had got too strong a hold on the soil for the planters' October indigo sowings to be carried out.

We must again beg our readers to endeavour to bring home to themselves this state of things, by imagining the whole rural population of Essex to have taken possession of the fields, driven the servants of the owners and landlords from them, and sown them down with crops of their own choosing, there being no redress to be got by application to the authorities beyond a reference to the Civil Courts—a tedious and expensive process, generally attended with success at a period too late for the proper agricultural operations of the year. This would be called a parody on Government in England, but it is what the English capitalist has to submit to, who has brought his funds for investment in Bengal.

"*Pubna*, Nov. 7.

" I AM sorry to have to inform you that the state of affairs here and the combination against the concern is as bad as ever, if not worse. There are some six individual heads of this combination; they have divided the concern between them, each collecting money from the Ryots of his division to enable him to carry on the war against my interest. They fine and maltreat any person who dares to enter any of my factories, and any Ryot who may come to see me is punished to the utmost extent. They have got large sums of money in this way, and, of course, the longer the quarrel lasts the better for them; so that I see no chance of a speedy termination to it. The heads of the combination have regular establishments of 'lattials,' who in open day go from village to village to punish any Ryot who may act contrary to orders. The poor they coerce with blows and by fines, and the more respectable portion of the people by preventing their getting food from the bazaars, not allowing a barber to approach their houses, insulting their women at the ghauts, beating their servants, &c.; so that all classes are compelled to act according to their orders and wishes, and we are helpless. No servant of mine dare go into any of my villages, talook, or izarah. No man will undertake the office of Tussildar. Trees are cut down by order of the heads of the combination, and sold to whoever will purchase them. New Ryots come in and put up houses on my lands wherever they please, and, instead of applying to me for leave to do so, they give 'nuzzurs' to the heads of the combination, and act according to their orders.

" On the 13th ult. some servants of mine gave evidence in an Act IV case before the magistrate at Koostiah. Their evidence was given about 3 p. m.; at 5 p. m., or two hours afterwards, their houses, eight miles distant from Koostiah, were plundered of everything they contained. The deputy magistrate went to their houses next day, and saw that they had been plundered, and got evidence to that effect. Whether the parties guilty of such an outrage will be punished or not remains to be seen.

" On the 4th inst. a Ryot complained to the magistrate that one of the heads of the combination had fined him 25 rupees; that the man in question, with a number of 'lattials,' surrounded his house and compelled him to pay the fine. On the following night the same party surrounded his house, broke into it, and took away his wife, his daughter, and his mother-in-law, himself escaping by mere chance. The magistrate investigated the matter yesterday, and the charge was proved.

" The great object of the Ryots just now appears to be that of preventing any of my old servants working for me, so that it is with great difficulty I can retain any of my office servants. I have got but three or four of them, all the rest having been compelled to leave. Three days ago, one of my most useful writers was obliged to leave, as the Ryots kept permanent guard over his house, so that his family were denied egress or ingress until he appeared and paid a fine for daring to work for me. No person who had not actually witnessed it could imagine the state of affairs in this neighbourhood. The authorities know all about it, but they are helpless, as, if crime is brought to their notice, the necessary evidence cannot be had—no man dare give it, even although he wished to. As to the native police they have an ample harvest time of it; the sums of money they are getting are almost incredible; their demands such as were never before heard of, even in Bengal: and I have no hesitation in saying that they extort more money in one month now-a-days, than they did during the whole of the ten years from 1850 to 1859 inclusive.

The amount due this concern by the Ryots on account of rents for the current year is upwards of 65,000 rupees. Of course, the whole of this may be collected through the Courts, but every suit instituted against a Ryot will but increase the ill-feeling between the tenantry and the concern, as paying rents with costs will fall heavily upon them.

" I have done and said all I possibly could to bring about an amicable arrangement. I have told every person, even some of the leaders of the combination, in presence of Mr. Bainbridge, that I don't want to sow Indigo just now, nor until the Ryots are willing to do so of their own accord, and that I merely want my rent; but it is not a mere Indigo quarrel just now—it is one of native against European; and the question is, whether we cannot be compelled to leave our factories altogether or not. My Ryots state openly that they will not pay rents, neither will they do work of any kind for a sahib, and that such will be the rule throughout the district in a short time.

" I daily receive petitions from Ryots who are unable to contend with their more powerful neighbours. The poor man's lands are forcibly taken possession of, and his crops cut and taken away. I am powerless and cannot help them, neither can the authorities, as they won't act in accordance with the laws; and who will bear witness to the fact? So hundreds of the poorer Ryots are being ruined. This state of affairs cannot last very long. Plunder, dacoity, and crime of every kind will become rife throughout the country; the idle and the wicked see that they can act as they please with impunity. They have done so for some months past, and as the year advances, and the necessaries of life become dearer, the district will become more and more disorganized, and the end will be that Government will have to resort to the strong hand sooner or later."

From the Calcutta Correspondent of the TIMES. *Printed in the* TIMES *of 14th January,* 1861.

I MUST allude for a few moments to that *vexata questio—* Indigo. On this point I can give you the opinion of a gentleman who is universally admitted to be the most practical civilian and the best administrator in Bengal—Mr. Yule, Commissioner of Bhagulpore. Mr. Yule has lately been engaged in investigating the circumstances under which in the month of May last the Ryots attacked the factory of Beniagram. Of this attack I gave a particular account at the time, and I stated that but for the noble defence of the agent, Mr. Lyon, the most disastrous results would have ensued. I referred also to the fact that, previously to the attack, not only had no assistance been rendered to Mr. Lyon by the magistrate of the

district, but that functionary had warned him that he would
hold him (Mr. Lyon) responsible for any disturbances that
might ensue. When the factory was attacked the anti-Indigo
faction loudly asserted that Mr. Lyon was an oppressor, and
that the attack was a natural consequence of his misdeeds. It
was useless to attempt to controvert this statement; every
office in the country was held by men pledged to oppose the
settlement of Europeans in the country, and they were able to
make their own statements. Now, however, the question may
be alluded to; it has been examined into by Mr. Yule, a
civilian, one of their own order, and this is what he says:—

"The reports show how the Ryots, at first amenable to
remonstrances from the police, gradually learned to disregard
them till they attacked Beniagram in open daylight, and in
defiance of a considerable police force present on the spot.
The Ryots appeared to have said all along that what they wanted
was a Hakim to inquire into their grievances, and the prisoners
in this case plainly told me that they never would have been
in the scrape they were, had a Hakim been at hand. I say the
same, and this belief renders the duty of passing sentence, at
all times a painful one, infinitely more so in this case than
usual. In conclusion, I must observe that Mr. Lyon by his
determined defence saved not only his own life and property,
but, had the attack on Beniagram been successful, every planter
and factory in this subdivision and Maldah would, I verily
believe, have been attacked, and there is no saying how far the
outbreak might have spread. Mr. Lyon had quelled the spirit
of destruction before almost it was known to be abroad."

He further acquits Mr. Lyon of oppression, and alludes
pointedly to the weak spot in our rule—to the real causes of all
the Indigo disturbances. These are, according to Mr. Yule,
inefficient magistrates, an utterly useless police, and the want
of summary courts of justice. These are the remedies he would
propose, and, by a coincidence not curious but striking, these
are the remedies which the planters have proposed, but which
the Lieutenant-Governor will not have. I must, however, do
Mr. Grant the justice to state, that since the publication in this
country of English opinion on the subject of Indigo the tone
of his letters has softened down. Within the last fortnight
two factories, belonging to Messrs. Watson, have been burnt
down, and rewards have been offered for the discovery and
apprehension of the offenders. Magistrates, also, have been
directed to bestir themselves, and put a stop to the crimes
which disgrace the districts. This spasmodic movement would
appear to be somewhat late in the day. An annual expendi-

ture of more than half a million sterling has been lost to the Ryots, and these, prompted by men behind the scenes, are endeavouring to make combinations for the avowed object of living at their ease without the obligation of industry and toil.

II.

Extracts from the HONOURABLE ASHLEY EDEN'S *Evidence before the Indigo Commission,* 1860.

3578. Mr. *Fergusson.*] In the forty-nine cases (of affrays) which you ferretted out, as having occurred during the last thirty years, is it not the case that in more than half of them, Europeans have not been accused, or, if accused, have been acquitted?—There are scarcely any one of these cases, in which the European or Principal Manager of the concern has ever been put upon his trial, although in many of them, the Judges trying the cases have expressed strong opinions that such Europeans were themselves implicated in them; and it is to this importunity and freedom from responsibility that I attribute the constant recurrence of these violent outrages.

3579. In such instances as you have mentioned, was it not a gross dereliction of duty on the part of the Government not to prosecute the Europeans?—There certainly was a failure of justice which, in my opinion, may, to a certain extent, be attributed to the strong bias, which the Governor and many of the officers of Government have always displayed in favour of those engaged in this particular cultivation; this may also partly have arisen from the difficulty which exists under the present law of obtaining a conviction against Europeans, as, for instance, in the case in which a planter, named Dick, *alias* Richard Aimes, was murdered by a European planter named Jones, a French planter named Pierre Aller, and some native servants, in which the Frenchman and the natives being amenable to the Courts of the country, were imprisoned for life; whilst Young, the European British subject, not being subject to the jurisdiction of the local Court, was tried in Her Majesty's Supreme Court in Calcutta, and was acquitted on precisely the same evidence as was brought against the foreigners and natives who were convicted in the district Court: the sentence being upheld by the Nizamut Adawlut.

3580. Then you consider that in that case justice was obtained in the Mofussil Courts and denied in the Supreme Court?—I consider that the Judges of the Court of the Nizamut Adawlut are fully as competent to come to a decision on the evidence before them, as a Calcutta petty Jury. I shall, therefore, consider that, in this instance, a failure of justice occurred in the Supreme Court.

3581. *If I tell you, that I was in the Supreme Court during the whole of that trial, and with a strong feeling against the prisoner, and that I, and most other gentlemen in Calcutta, considered it impossible to find him guilty on the evidence, would it alter your opinion in any manner?—NO, as with those facts before them, and commenting on those facts, the Sudder Court subsequently convicted the remainder of that party as accessories to the murder on that evidence; the previous acquittal in the Supreme Court, and the distrust thrown upon the evidence having been urged by the defendant's Counsel, and over-ruled. Moreover, if the murder was not committed, where is Dick alias Richard Aimes, who has never appeared since.*

3606. Mr. Fergusson.] *In the present state of the Mofussil Courts and with the present Judges who preside in them, would you like to see any European friend tried in them?—I think that if the Courts are good enough for the natives, they are good enough for Europeans. If they are not good enough for natives, they are not fit to have any jurisdiction at all over any one. As far as I am myself concerned, I would sooner be tried, if innocent, in the local Sessions Courts, with an appeal to the Nizamut, than in the Supreme Court. If guilty, I would prefer the Supreme Court and a Calcutta jury.*

3664. Mr. *Fergusson.*] Then you do not think that the residence of European gentlemen in the interior has improved either the physical or moral condition of the people?—*Although I have no doubt, that there are many individuals who have done great good and rendered assistance to the authorities, yet, as a general rule, I do not think the residence of Indigo Planters has improved to any great extent the physical or moral condition of the people.** I believe there are to be found more bad characters settled around Indigo Factories, than in distant villages in which an European has never been seen. My remarks do not apply either to silk manufacturers, or rum distillers, or Sunderbund settlers; of the latter of whom I had a great many in my

---

* Here Mr. Eden, the *Bengal civilian*, differs from the Statesmen Lord William Bentinck and Sir Charles Metcalfe, whose opinions are cited at page 18.

district; but against whom I never had a single complaint. I allude only to the Indigo Planters, who, as a rule, live in constant antagonism with the people around them; a state of things which cannot conduce to the peace of the country.

III.

Petition of the INDIGO PLANTERS' ASSOCIATION *to* LORD CANNING *against the* HONOURABLE J. P. GRANT.

To the Right Honourable his Excellency the Viceroy and Governor-General of India in Council.

The humble Petition of the Bengal Indigo Planters' Association.

RESPECTFULLY SHEWETH,

THAT your Petitioners' Association is composed principally of persons engaged in the cultivation of Indigo in the Lower Provinces of Bengal, a cultivation which has been by one Right Honourable Member of the Council remarked upon as one of the few in India attracting British capital to native labour, and one which the Government would above all others wish to encourage.

That although your petitioners are convinced of this desire on the part of the Government of India, the present Governor of Bengal, the Honourable John Peter Grant, has since his appointment to his present office unfortunately acted in such a way as to throw nearly the whole of the Indigo districts, and especially Kishnaghur, into confusion, and unless something be done to remedy the present system of misrule, many Indigo Planters must be irretrievably ruined, while the inevitable result of the withdrawal of British capital from the districts is a matter of no small importance.

That your Excellency in Council may probably be, in consequence of your Excellency's duties having made it necessary for you to proceed up the country at the time in question, not minutely acquainted with the origin of the disturbances which have for some months been existing in Kishnaghur and the adjacent districts, and which have already put Government to so much expense.

That the origin of those disturbances undoubtedly was the conduct of the Honourable Mr. Eden, then magistrate of

Baraset, in allowing the Ryots of the Baraset district to become
aware that his feeling was against the Indigo Planters, where-
upon the manager of the Bengal Indigo Company complained
to the then Governor of Bengal now Sir Frederick Halliday,
but that gentleman having retired from office, the matter was
finally investigated by the Honourable John Peter Grant, who
supported Mr. Eden.

That on the 17th August, 1859, the Honourable Mr. Eden
wrote to the deputy magistrate of Kallaroah a letter, which
your Excellency in Council will at once see was intended to
point out the advisability of Ryots objecting to cultivate.

From

> The Honourable A. EDEN,
> *Magistrate at Baraset,*

To

> Baboo HEMCHUNDER KUR,
> *Deputy Magistrate, Kalaroah Sub-Division.*

Sir,

As the cultivation of Indigo is carried on to a considerable
extent in your sub-division, I beg to forward for your information and guidance extracts from a letter No. 4516, dated
21st July, 1859, from the Secretary to the Government of
Bengal to the Commissioner of the Nuddea Division.

You will perceive that the course laid down for the police in
Indigo disputes, is to protect the Ryot in the possession of his
lands, on which he is at liberty to sow any crop he likes,
without any interference on the part of the Planter or any one
else. The Planter is not at liberty, under pretext of the Ryots
having promised to sow Indigo for him, to enter forcibly upon
the land of the Ryot. Such promises can only be produced
against the Ryot in the Civil Court, and the magisterial authorities have nothing to do with them, for there must be two
parties to a promise; and it is possible that the Ryots, whose
promises or contracts are admitted, may still have many irresistible pleas to avoid the consequence the Planter insists upon.

That on the 20th August, 1859, the said Hemchunder Kur
published in the district the following unfortunate and ill-
judged proclamation:—

Translation.

"To the Darogah of Thannah Kalarooah. Take notice.—
A letter from the Magistrate of Baraset, dated the 17th
August, 1859, having been received, accompanied by an extract

from an English letter from the Secretary to the Government of Bengal, to the address of the Commissioner of the Nuddea Division, dated 21st July, 1859, No. 4516, to the following purport, that in cases of disputes relating to Indigo Ryots they shall retain possession of their own lands, and shall sow on them what crops they please, and the police will be careful that no Indigo Planter nor any one else be able to interfere in the matter, and Indigo Planters shall not be able forcibly to cause Indigo to be sown on the lands of those Ryots on the ground that the Ryots consented to the sowing, &c., of Indigo. If Ryots have so consented, the Indigo Planter may bring an action against them in the Civil Court. The Criminal Court has no concern in these matters, because, notwithstanding such contracts, or such consent withheld or given, Ryots may urge unanswerable excuses against the sowing of Indigo. A copy of Perwannah is therefore issued, and you are requested in future to act accordingly.—Dated 20th August, 1859."

That the consequence of this was that the Ryots in that and the surrounding districts immediately believed that Government wished to put a stop to Indigo planting, and on the 14th October, 1859, the manager of the Jingergatcha Indigo concern brought to the Commissioner's notice the dangerous effects of such a proclamation, and after an investigation, the Commissioner, Mr. Grote, as well as Messrs. Reid and Drummond, who were all men who thoroughly understood the Indigo districts and the people, unanimously condemned the indiscretion of the magistrate and deputy magistrate, although the Honourable Mr. Grant, on the 7th April, 1860, wrote a letter in which he stated that he considered that Mr. Eden had given a satisfactory explanation.

That although that might appear so to his Honour, the consequences in the meantime were serious in the extreme to the Planters; and about the beginning of February, on the return of the Honourable Mr. Grant from a tour through the Indigo districts, a report spread rapidly throughout the whole of the villages that the Government were opposed to the cultivation of Indigo.

That your petitioners believe that this was caused by the Lieutenant-Governor allowing himself to form and openly express an opinion hostile to the system of Indigo planting, although at a subsequent interview which a deputation of your petitioners' Association had with his Honour, he stated plainly that he had never had any experience in the Indigo districts, and that he was very ignorant on the subject; and in order to show that your petitioners' belief on that subject is not unfounded, they would beg your Excellency's attention to the following extract from a letter from Mr. Grant to Mr. Sconce, dated 23rd March, 1860, written ten days after the interview with the deputation, and published by the authority of the Government of Bengal, which is as follows :

" I am myself of opinion that the Indigo cultivators " (meaning the Ryots)—" have and long have had great and increasing ground of just complaint against the whole system of Indigo cultivation."

That the occasion of the writing of that letter was the earnest entreaty of the Planters that His Honor should request Mr. Sconce to bring into the Legislative Council a bill to compel Ryots to complete their engagements, a measure which was absolutely necessary, as from the rapid spread of the disaffection amongst the Ryots many Planters saw ruin staring them in the face, while the districts were becoming so disturbed that neither life nor property were safe.

That the Legislative Council at once saw the necessity of speedy action, and the Act XI of 1860 was passed and received your Excellency's assent.

That your petitioners believe that if the local authorities had been permitted to carry out the provisions of this Act without interference on the part of His Honor the Lieutenant-Governor, none of the difficulties with which the Planters have to contend would now exist, while instead of having a prospect before them of utter ruin to many factories next season, matters would have gone on to the mutual advantage of the capitalist and labourer —all differences between them being settled like every other commercial arrangement upon the simple question of price.

That immediately upon the Act being passed, His Honor published on the 4th April, 1860, a letter of instructions which is hereto annexed and marked No. 1, which refers to a previous letter published by His Honor, and which is hereto annexed and marked No. 2, and your petitioners humbly submit to your Excellency in Council that at a time when the Ryots were all under the belief that the Lieutenant-Governor was opposed to the system of Indigo planting, it would have been more proper to leave the magisterial officers to exercise their own discretion as to the mode of acquainting the Ryots with the terms of the Act, instead of directing the magistrates to communicate to them the desire of Government, or pointing out to them as in the 7th paragraph of the letter marked No. 2, that the Act was only to apply to the current season, thereby keeping alive in the minds of the Ryots a feeling of excitement that a discreet magistrate if left to himself would have known how to avoid.

That considering the powers which His Honour has as to the removal of magistrates, it was as your petitioners submit uncalled for—unless the Honourable Lieutenant-Governor could not trust the magisterial officers of the district—to hold out as he did in the letter No. 1 a threat of removal if any magistrate interpreted the Act contrary to His Honour's views.

That the Lieutenant-Governor in laying down rules for the interpretation of the Act exceeded, as your petitioners submit, his powers and trespassed upon the province of the Legislative Council and of the judicial officers of the Government, because where a question as to the meaning of an Act arose, a judicial tribunal where both sides could be heard, was the proper forum to interpret it.

That your petitioners beg to draw to the earnest consideration of your Excellency in Council that the Lieutenant-Governor has since that Act was passed, interfered with the working of it in such a way as to make it wholly useless for the purpose which the Legislative Council had in view, and your petitioners have only to refer to the records of the Government of Bengal containing the papers relative to Indigo planting which are published by authority, to shew that His Honour has exercised an improper and most indiscreet interference with sentences passed by the magistrates.

That soon after the passing of the Act a Mooktear was tried by Mr. Betts for instigating Ryots to break their engagements, and a number of Ryots were sentenced for ploughing up Indigo that had been sown.

That both of these offences had become very common, and it was necessary for the sake of example to put them down at once; but notwithstanding this and the express provision by the Legislative Council that there should be no appeal, the Lieutenant-Governor, on the 19th April, 1860, ordered the Commissioner to review these proceedings as appears by the letter hereto annexed and marked No. 3.

That by adopting such a course the prosecutors had not even the chance which, if there had been an appeal, they would have had, of showing that the convictions were proper, and the Lieutenant-Governor soon afterwards ordered the release of the Mooktear and the Ryots, which did more harm than your Excellency can imagine.

That in order to show what the wish of His Honour was, this proceeding has been followed up by his directing the release of many other Ryots imprisoned duly according to law, and the removal from the Indigo districts of the Magistrates, Messrs. Betts, Mackenzie, Macniell and Taylor, and the substitution for

N

them, in cases coming under the new Act, of some of the Principal Sudder Ameens of other districts.

That the effect of His Honour's interference has, amongst other things, been to create an impression not only in the minds of the magistrates but also of the Planters and Ryots, that any decisions in favour of the Planters would meet with the disapproval of the Government of Bengal, and your petitioners would beg leave to draw the attention of your Excellency in Council to the evidence amongst others of Mr. Forlong and Mr. Taylor, given before the Indigo Commissioners (the evidence on oath of men of the most unimpeachable character) to shew the effect of these acts of His Honour and the absurdity of continuing to institute suits under the new Act.

That in a recent case in which a decision has been given by Mr. Herschell, magistrate of Kishnaghur, which your petitioners consider to be entirely contrary to the evidence, and most unjust to the Planter concerned, His Honour has, upon a special report of the case to him, ordered copies of it to be distributed among the officials before whom cases under Act XI, 1860, are tried, with an intimation that Mr. Herschell's decision is to be taken as a rule to guide them in all similar cases. This your petitioners look upon as a most unusual and unauthorized interference with the ordinary course of law, and the proper independence of the judicial authorities, and especially unfair and injurious to your petitioners, inasmuch as the evidence produced was chiefly that of books and documents, kept according to the common practice of all Indigo factories, which are thereby and in this particular case unjustly condemned wholesale as not to be received as good evidence of claims against Ryots, and being the only corroborative evidence Planters have to produce, such claims are practically rendered impossible of proof.

That your petitioners beg to draw particular attention to the evidence of Mr. Taylor, a man of the highest honour and reputation, (given before the Commissioners,) by which it appears that while the decision of cases under Act XI, was left to the gentlemen acting as magistrates in the district, every case was decided in his favour, but every case which has since their removal been brought by him before the principal Sudder Ameen, although supported by the same class of evidence as in the previous cases, has been dismissed,—a fact that as your petitioners submit shews the effect of the interference which they now complain of.

That in several districts contracts have been entered into for three years and upwards, and in the absence of any Legislative enactment to the contrary, such contracts are in every way binding, and many Planters have made their calculations for the several seasons on the knowledge of these contracts; but His Honour, without taking this consideration, or indeed considering for one instant the serious effect on all cultivators of Indigo of such a proceeding, lately published a proclamation, the immediate effect of which was, to cause the Ryots in many districts, who were previously perfectly quiet, and especially in Messrs. Watson and Co.'s factories, to combine against their employers.

That the proclamation is as follows;—

Istahar by the order of the Honourable the Lieutenant-Governor.

The following Istahar is issued for the information of those Ryots who have been put in prison on account of claims against them for non-fulfilment of their contracts for sowing indigo or having taking advances for the current season, and those against whom claims are now pending, as also those who are in any way connected with Indigo.

The Act XI of 1860, respecting Indigo, which is now in force will only remain so for a short time. Commissioners will be appointed before the commencement of next season for sowing Indigo to enquire into the cause of complaint by the Ryots in respect of the cultivation of Indigo, and on their report to Government, such rules will be laid down as will benefit all parties, and will undoubtedly show no partiality to any one. On the expiration of the present season it will be optional for the Ryots to receive advances and to enter into contracts for sowing Indigo. That is to say, that as for those who have been imprisoned for not sowing Indigo this season in terms of their contract on proved claims, it will rest with them to receive or not receive advances to sow Indigo in future, although for this season they are required in terms of their contract to sow Indigo.

Revenue Commissioner's Office.
Nuddea Division. }

That if there were any doubt in the mind of your Excellency in Council as to the views of His Honour on the subject of the Indigo disputes and his interference with and implied disapproval of the Act of the Legislative Council, this proclamation would, as your petitioners believe, remove it, and the effect of it upon the contracts not yet completed will be irretrievably injurious. That in consequence of this constant interference of His Honour, the people of Lower Bengal are losing all respect for the officers of Government, and the minds of the people in the Indigo districts are kept in a state of greater excitement and uncertainty than they were before Act XI of 1860 was passed. The districts of Jessore and Pubna, hitherto comparatively quiet, are becoming seriously disturbed, and in them as well as in Kishnaghur, the greatest difficulty is experienced by Planters in inducing the Ryots to cut the fine crop of Indigo plant now ripe for manufacture, and which will give a handsome return to both Planters and Ryots, unless allowed to perish by the misguided folly of the people.

That although in the course of the evidence taken under the Commission appointed to enquire into the state of the cultivation of Indigo, and which Commission was appointed at the earnest request of your petitioners, a mass of evidence in support of the allegations that the Ryots are opposed to the cultivation of Indigo, and that it is anything but advantageous to the people to have it cultivated has been given, your petitioners refer with confidence to the evidence of the Planters themselves, and more particularly to the plain, visible and undeniable fact that wherever Indigo factories are situated in Bengal, there the people are richer, the country more highly cultivated, and the province in a more advanced and prosperous state that in any district where factories do not exist; and your petitioners point with pride to the fact, that within but a few years, miles and miles of country which were covered with the rankest jungle, are now highly cultivated and productive lands.

That your petitioners believe that if your Excellency in Council is desirous of retaining English capital in Bengal, it is absolutely necessary to adopt some measures to prevent his Honour, the Lieutenant-Governor of Bengal, from interfering as he now does, behind the backs of persons interested, in cases pending or decided, with the due administration of the law, and to direct his Houour to leave to the Legislature and the regularly appointed tribunals of the country, the promulgation and administration of the law.

> Your Petitioners therefore humbly pray your Excellency in Council to take into consideration this petition, and to pass such orders as may oblige his Honour, the Lieutenant-Governor of Bengal, to refrain from pursuing a course of conduct which cannot but be ruinous to the Indigo Planters in Bengal, and to point out to his Honour the impropriety of interfering with the due course of the administration of the law by the

regularly appointed judicial officers as laid down by the Legislative Council of India, and which interference is, as your petitioners submit, both illegal and unconstitutional, and especially indiscreet in the case of a dispute between capital and labour, and that your Excellency may pass such further orders as may under the above circumstances seem proper.

Dated 26th July, 1860.

IV.

Reply of the INDIGO PLANTERS' ASSOCIATION *to* MR. GRANT.

" *Calcutta,* Oct. 13.

" THE Committee of the Indigo Planters' Association having at last received from the Commissioner of Nuddea information which they requested from him on the 7th ult., they proceed to submit to his Excellency the Governor-General of India in Council the following remarks on the Minute of the Lieutenant-Governor of Bengal dated the 17th of August, which was communicated to the Association with your letter of August 31.

" Although his Excellency has expressed himself satisfied with Mr. Grant's explanations except on one point, the Committee respectfully beg to observe that Mr. Grant's Minute is not accompanied by any particulars of the cases to which he refers, by which his Excellency's judgment might be guided; and they, therefore, beg to submit the fullest details which they have been able to obtain in explanation. In commenting upon his Honour's Minute, the Committee are desirous of avoiding as much as possible anything like entering into a controversy with the Lieutenant-Governor; still they cannot but express their regret, that the tone of his Honour's Minute is such as to show how deeply his feelings are affected against the system of Indigo planting generally, and the persons who are engaged in that cultivation.

" In support of this position the Committee content themselves by simply referring his Excellency to the style, as well as the matter, of one paragraph only—namely, the 5th, which assumes as a granted fact that planters have been in the habit of committing every description of crime and oppression.

" The Committee do not wish either to enter into an argument as to the correctness of the Lieutenant-Governor's views of the position of the Ryot as a capitalist, as they believe that such a theory is one wholly new, and one particularly opposed to the general idea of what constitutes a Ryot in Bengal; but they must not be considered as in any way agreeing in the view his Honour takes of this subject, or assenting to his discovery, that the Ryot is a capitalist as distinguished from a labourer.

" The Committee would, however, draw particular attention to one part of the Minute, where the Lieutenant-Governor is obliged to confess that the gentlemen he employed in the judicial offices in the disturbed districts were unfit for the common duties of their stations, and the Committee think that such a confession from such authority must necessarily draw the attention of the Executive Government to the necessity of establishing such a system as will give the people a more efficient class of judicial officers; and the Committee would beg attention to this part of his Honour's Minute as supporting the truth of what has long been put forward by the planters as their most serious grievance—viz., the inefficient state of the Mofussil Courts. His Excellency will have an opportunity in a later part of this letter of judging of the fitness for the judicial bench of one of them (Mr. J. S. Bell), who is considered by his Honour as so much superior to the covenanted magistrates whom he superseded in their duties.

" The Committee consider it as hardly worth while referring to the earnest manner in which the Lieutenant-Governor argues as to there being no 'confusion' in the districts; they can only say that a publication of the Lieutenant-Governor's, dated the 17th of September, has led them to believe that the word 'confusion' was not strong enough to express the state of the district; and they believe that the mere fact of a vast military force being employed in that part of the country, where troops have not been stationed since it came under the British rule, proves 'confusion;' and they cannot but express their surprise that, at a time when all residents of these districts knew that affairs were daily becoming worse, his Honour should, as he does in the last paragraph of his Minute, refer to the crisis having passed over so peacefully, and with so little injury to the great interest at stake. The Committee can only say that the great interest of the European settler is for the present entirely ruined, and they see but little prospect of European capital being again embarked in the districts of Lower Bengal.

" But, leaving the general tenor of the Minute, the Committee would beg his Excellency's attention to the prominent cases brought forward by the Lieutenant-Governor, on which he lays much stress; and when the Committee show that his Honour has taken statements for granted without fully investigating the cases on which he relies, to found most severe remarks and attacks, not only on the planters, but on his own judicial officers, the Committee believe that his Excellency will attach much less weight to the Minute in question than at first sight would appear to be due to it.

" In the 28th paragragh of the Minute the Lieutenant-Governor refers to the case of the Mooktear who was, as stated in the planter's petition, sentenced by Mr. Betts to imprisonment and a fine for instigating Ryots not to sow.

It would naturally be supposed from the comments upon this case that the man in question, Teetaram Chuckerbutty, was a Mooktear acting as such on behalf of Ryots, and that he was sentenced for exercising his lawful avocations as a Mooktear; and his Honour, on this assumption, would make out that the sentence in question deprived the Ryots of legal assistance, and that it was intended to give an advantage to the planters.

The Committee have, however, ascertained that the man, though entitled, perhaps, to call himself a Mooktear, was, in fact, but an Omedwar (one seeking employment); that he had never appeared before Mr. Betts as Mooktear; that he was not employed in any way by any Ryot on that occasion; that a few days previously he had waited on Mr. Forlong, begging for employment in any capacity; and that on the day in question he was hanging about Mr. Betts's tent, looking out for the chance of anything that might occur, holding no Mooktearnama; and, in fact, the Ryots whose cases were before Mr. Betts never consulted him, or referred to him as their legal adviser.

" Mr. Betts had for more than two hours been patiently explaining to the Ryots their position and liabilities, pointing out to them that the law distinctly laid it down that if they did not complete their contracts they would be subject to imprisonment, and perhaps be cast in damages, and he begged them to retire and think over the matter.

" To the former alternative the Ryots were inclined to agree, and they retired to some neighbouring trees to consult. The man Teetaram Chuckerbutty went to them then for the first time, and, joining in their conversation, advised them to resist sowing, and not to mind the consequences. Information of this was brought to Mr. Betts, who at once had him brought into court, heard the evidence, and, finding that he was not

acting as Mooktear for any of the parties, convicted him of
instigating, with evil design, the Ryots not to sow.

"The Committee admit that the sentence might not perhaps have been strictly legal within the words of the section
of the Act as amended and passed, but the mere fact of an
error as to the interpretation of the wording of the Act has a
very different effect from that which the Lieutenant-Governor
attributes to this decision, which he erroneously regards as
a gross interference with the liberty of the legal agent of the
Ryots.

"His Honour is wholly misinformed as to the Ryots in
that quarter not being able to obtain the services of legal
agents to defend their cases, and it is wholly incorrect to state
'that the prosecutors for several days had it all their own way;'
so far from this being the case, on the very same day, a complaint having been lodged against one really acting as a
Mooktear before Mr. Betts, it was at once dismissed by him,
on the ground that he could not interfere with the advice that
any legal agent deemed it right to give to his client, and
Mr. Betts distinctly pointed out to the complainants that the
position of this man was wholly different from that of Teetaram
Chuckerbutty.

"The Committee unhesitatingly refer to the records of the
Court in proof of their assertion that no Mooktear was deterred
from representing Ryots in consequence of Mr. Betts's decision,
and they are quite at a loss to understand upon whose representation the Lieutenant-Governor has been led into so grave
an error; and his Excellency will see how serious a matter this
is when he observes the frequent and bitter allusions to it in
the Minute.

"The other case on which his Honour comments, as
showing not only misconduct on the part of Mr. Betts, but,
what is of far more importance to the Committee, as supporting
the grave charges of forgery and perjury against a planter, or,
at any rate, against their subordinates is that mentioned in
paragraph 32, which he says accidentally came to his knowledge,
as one in which Mr. Betts gave a planter a decree against a
Ryot on a written agreement, purporting to have been made in
1856, though executed on stamped paper which on inspection
proved to have been sold in 1859.

"On investigation this charge proves to be utterly untrue.

"The Koboolyat or agreement in question, of which a copy
and translation is herewith sent, recites that the Ryot (Hishab-
dee Shaik Mundle) who was complained against, was indebted
to the factory at the close of the season 1859, to the extent of

3r. 3a. 6p. ; that he had received a further advance of 12r. in cash in consideration of his engaging to cultivate seven beegahs with Indigo in 1860, and in the four following years terminating in 1864, the correctness of the account showing the balance of 3r. 3a. 6p., and the payment of the advance of 12r. in cash, was sworn to by the manager of the factory, Mr. Taylor, and proved by Mr. Betts's inspection of the books, and on that evidence Mr. Betts gave the decree against the Ryot on the 18th of April, 1860, and the Committee would draw particular attention to the different years mentioned in that document as those over which the contract was to extend.

"On the 27th of July, 1860, Mr. Principal Sudder Ameen Bell, who is above referred to, as being considered superior to the other magistrates, on hearing another case, delivered the judgment, of which a copy is herewith sent, and to which we beg his Excellency's particular attention, as his Excellency will perceive in that judgment he did refer to the Koboolyat filed in the former case, which is above referred to, and apparently without having made any further inquiries, and certainly without having read the document which, in fact, was not in evidence before him, he gratuitously pronounced the same to be a spurious exhibit, in as much as it is dated at the foot, in figures, December, 1856, when the stamp was sold in November, 1859.

"The Committee beg his Excellency's attention to the Koboolyat, which requires only the slightest glance to show that the date of the English year 1856 is only a mistake and clerical error of the Bengalee writer, and that it was a Koboolyat for season 1860 to 1864 inclusive, and that the whole text and wording of the agreement unquestionably prove this to be the case. When an error was made in one of Mr. Herschel's Purwannahs, that of the 19th of April, which caused the planters' losses, that can only be estimated by tens of thousands of pounds, and Mr. Herschel put forward, as his defence, that it was a clerical mistake, and that it was by accident that the obnoxious copy happened to go to the only place where it was likely to do harm, the planters did not refuse to accept the explanation, however opposed to probability.

"It would seem, however, that no such feelings of fairness are to be evinced by the authorities towards planters, and that no opportunity is to be omitted to misrepresent and malign them, and this is particularly the case in the present instance, where the record could have at once been called for and inspected, and which in fairness ought to have been done.

" The Committee can only hope that neither Mr. Bell himself, whom the Lieutenant-Governor designates as the experienced Civil Judge : Mr. Herschel, the magistrate, who eagerly seized on the case, and sent it up; Mr. Lushington the Commissioner who reported it to the Lieutenant-Governor; nor Mr. Grant himself ever looked at the document before basing on it the grave charges that are contained in the Minute. Five minutes' inspection would have prevented a most unjust accusation being put forward in an official document, and much of that official document would then have been unwritten.

" In para. 357, his Honour, on whom this case seems to have made much impression, again introduces the Koboolyat as the foundation of a sarcasm, and a slander on the whole body of planters, in the following words :—

"' It must doubtless have been agreeable to planters when their suits were tried on such a fashion, that decrees were obtainable on agreements purporting to be four years old, though written on stamps which were in the vendors' shops one year ago.'

" The Committee respectfully, but most earnestly, beg to submit to his Excellency that such language is as unworthy of a man holding Mr. Grant's high official position as it has now been proved to be unfounded and unjust; and should his Excellency (as they cannot but believe he will), view the matter in the same light as they do, they appeal to his high sense of honour and fairness to point out to the Lieutenant-Governor the propriety of withdrawing the charge as publicly as it has been made.

" In the 37th para., his Honour replies to the complaint that was made, of his influencing the minds of judicial officers by circulating to all in the districts copy of a decision of Mr. Herschel, and of a letter from Mr. Lushington on the subject of a charge against the servants of a factory, respecting which Mr. Herschel had at that time made a preliminary inquiry.

" The communications referred to are annexed, and the Committee appeal to his Lordship in Council to say if they are not of a nature to prejudice all magistrates against planters.

" The Committee have carefully gone into the case referred to, which was sent up for trial to the judge, whose decision was adverse, to the servants of the factory; but the Committee do not hesitate to declare their belief that the decision is incorrect; that it was biassed by the proceedings of the Lieutenant-Governor; that it will be reversed on appeal; and if Government will publish Mr. Lushington's communications, the proprietors of the concern are prepared to prosecute for a libel, with the object of proving that the allegations are unfounded and untrue.

"Beyond defending the body they represent from the grave and sweeping charges brought against them by the Lieutenant-Governor, the Committee do not desire to contest, or to enter into a controversy on individual cases, but they feel it their duty to protest on constitutional grounds against the interference of the Lieutenant-Governor, which has unquestionably been exercised to such an extent as to impair, if not to destroy, judicial independence within the districts under his control. His Excellency will find, on inquiry, that upon the abolition of the office of Superintendent of Police, an officer who, from his position, could not be classed with that of the Lieutenant-Governor, or be considered as having any such influence as that of the head of the Government, the supervising control over the proceedings of magistrates, pending or disposed of, rests in the hands of the Lieutenant-Governor of Bengal; and the Committee respectfully submit that such a power exercised as it is by Mr. Grant, who is superior to the whole Judicial Bench of Bengal, and who has complete power over the members of that body, is one that is dangerous to the true interests of justice, and one that ought not to exist, more especially so when the uncovenanted officers of that body are completely under the control and hold their offices subject to the pleasure of the Lieutenant-Governor alone.

"In thus replying to his Honour's minute, the Committee have avoided as much as possible acting otherwise than in a calm spirit; but although they feel that they are contending with one whose position makes it impolitic on their part to enter into controversy with him, they cannot consistently with their duty, or feeling as English gentlemen, representing a large European Association, composed of many men who have not only invested their all in this country, but have done so in the belief that they would be protected by the leading principles of an European Government, allow such serious charges as these brought by his Honour to pass unremarked upon, and without protesting against the injustice and impropriety of them as they now do; and, believing that a different line of conduct on the part of the Government of Bengal would have led to a very different result to that which now exists, they submit these remarks to his Excellency, trusting that this matter is one of sufficient importance to attract to its careful consideration his Excellency's earnest attention."

V.

Latest accounts contained in the " Friend of India," the " Bengal Hurkaru," and the " Calcutta Englishman."

(From the " Friend of India," November 29.)

GOVERNMENT BY ABSTRACT PRINCIPLES. — Logical government, like logical theology, is a dangerous mistake in practical life. Admirable as systems, both fail when applied to men with more passion than intellect, whose habits are the result of centuries of growth, whose beliefs are narrow and one-sided, whose rights stretch far back beyond the widest statute of limitation, whose prejudices must be allowed to perish as slowly as they have been permitted to grow. The doctrine of predestination may be logically true, but the consciousness of man tells him that his will is free. The abominations of slavery may be most patent, but the well-being of society demanded a gradual emancipation of the slave, and the indemnification of his master. The evils of the system of Indigo cultivation which the East India Company created may be great, and the logical course is certainly to put an end to them at once and for ever. But the good of the cultivator, the rights of the Planter, the general quiet of the country, and the claims of commerce, all demand that the evils be removed by a reformation which will improve the system or render a better possible, not by a revolution which will destroy it and sow the seeds of a jacquerie.

What Government by abstract principles has done for Lower Bengal may be seen in the present state of the four rich districts of Jessore, Nuddea, Pubna, and Furredpore. We have been at the pains to make out a list of all the Indigo " Concerns" which have this year been suddenly and violently ruined. An unwillingness to disclose the private affairs of individual Planters prevents us from giving the names in detail, but the results of the list now before us are in the gross sufficiently startling. They agree in all main points with those given by the Indigo Commission in their Report. On 1st October, 1859, there were in these four districts 27 Concerns, each consisting of a large number of factories, valued in the gross at £1,244,000, or about a million and a quarter sterling. Of this there is no doubt, as several of them are mortgaged to within a narrow margin of the values assigned. Their yearly outlay, of which the greater portion was spent in the agricultural districts, was £400,000, or nearly half a million sterling. For the past eight years the books of the Calcutta

Indigo brokers show that these 27 Concerns have manufactured 25,165 maunds of the finest Indigo, which has been sold at the average price of Rs. 210 the 82 lbs. In London the average cost has been Rs. 4 a pound. Up to this moment there is no prospect of these factories turning out one pound of Indigo next season. If put up in the market the property would not realize any price whatever. The proprietors are ruined, and at least 30 lakhs which they have hitherto put in circulation among the Ryots every year are withdrawn. Admitting that the Planter ought to have met by anticipating the storm, admitting that the whole difficulty is one of price, and that in a few months the exasperation of the peasant will cease if he is attracted to grow the plant by being paid a fair value, what are we to say of the policy which has so worked as at once and violently to cause this ruin, and whose only panacea for the evil is—more Moonsiffs?

Mr. Grant has shown a laudable zeal in answering the attacks of the Indigo Planters, in meeting sarcasm by sarcasm, charge by counter-charge, complaints by sneers. His answer to the last defence of the Planters on the subject of the forged contract was sent in to Government a week ago. But as yet ill-judged proclamations, fruitful in adding fuel to the discontent which pervades Lower Bengal, are the only result of the Report of the Indigo Commission. In vain has the Government of India called on him for his Minute on that Report. In vain has a Bill been hurried through the Legislative Council to allow the local governments to establish Small Cause Courts in the disturbed districts. In vain has the Supreme Council voted money for their establishment. Mr. Grant does not approve of Small Cause Courts. He believes only in Moonsiffs with a regular gradation of appeal up to the Sudder and the Privy Council. The only excitement we give to the Bengali is litigation, and he does not wish to deprive him of that luxury. He cannot allow the establishment of courts in the Indigo districts with so large a jurisdiction as to Rs. 500, from which there is no appeal, with which he therefore cannot interfere. But as the Act has been passed he must do something. And so he resolves to establish four Small Cause Courts, in the suburbs of Calcutta, in Akyab, Dacca, and Moorshedabad. He has recommended two grades of judges, on Rs. 700 and Rs. 1,000 a month. As to the Indigo districts where the courts are really wanted at once he thus calculates. In the districts of Jessore and Nuddea there are 19 Moonsiffs. Each court must have a jurisdiction not larger than that of two Moonsiffs. This would give 10 Small Cause Courts to the two

districts, and where are judges or money for them to be found?
Instead of this he proposes to direct the Moonsiffs to arrange
their cases so that they shall devote three days a week to all
bond, debt, and minor suits, and three days to those of greater
duration and importance. The Appellate Courts are to do the
same, and this is Mr. Grant's reform in the Indigo districts.
A reform on the present system it is, but as ineffectual for the
object in view as a drop of water to extinguish Vesuvius.
The Planters want Small Cause Courts, the Supreme Government have ordered them, the public are convinced of their
utility. Let Mr. Grant for once throw over his abstract principles, and give them what they want. One judge like Mr.
Montriou in Jessore, and another in Kishnaghur, will give all
classes the chief, speedy, and effectual justice for which they
vainly cry.

(" *Bengal Hurkaru,*" *8th December,* 1860.)

INDIGO CULTIVATION.—We publish under the head of
Official Papers a correspondence which points out how wholly
the Government, the magistrates, and the police are answer-
able for the worst of the riots that have taken place with regard
to Indigo cultivation. It is only after a lapse of time that
Planters can prove how false are the accusations of their
calumniators, among whom the chief is the head of the Government, Mr. John Peter Grant. It was only after some among
them had been held up to the scorn of the world by that
gentleman as habitual forgers for about two months, that they
were enabled to prove that the charge was as false as malicious.
Mr. Grant also, in a note to one of his minutes, accused Mr.
Hampton of the Pubna district as guilty of a grave outrage of
which he has now been fully acquitted and the crime saddled
upon the police. Messrs. Eden and Herschel in their evidence
before the Indigo Commission both accused the Messrs. Lyon
of being oppressive planters. Mr. Herschel told us that he
was not "surprised at the attack upon Beniagram, as the
concern of which that factory forms a part, both on the Moorshedabad and Malda side of the river, has for many years past,
been the scene of the gravest outbreaks on the part of the
Ryots that he has seen in any district." Mr. Eden says that
the Aurungabad sub-division was established on account of the
oppression to which the people were subjected by the servants
of the Messrs. Lyon's factories. In opposition to the testimony
of these precocious young gentlemen we have the following

testimony of the magistrate who was deputed to investigate all the charges which the Messrs. Lyon's Ryots could bring against them, after they had been exasperated to the utmost by the result of the battle of Beniagram and while they were acting under the influence of a Dhurmoghut or religious conspiracy against them :—

" In conclusion I beg to state that no serious charges of any kind were brought before me against Mr. Lyon, by any of the accused concerned in the attack on the Beniagram Factory, neither am I aware that Mr. Lyon has in any way, personally maltreated his Ryots. Petty cases of exactions and ill treatment on the part of his factory subordinates were at times brought to his notice, and instead of at once taking up such himself, or referring complaints to our Courts, he would make them over to his Sudder Office Amlah, by whom some cases were sometimes hushed up, or misrepresented to Mr Lyon and redress not always given the aggrieved parties. None of these however were of so serious a nature as would have given rise to feelings which would have produced the occurrence that has been the subject of this enquiry. Since the institution of Act XI, of 1860, Mr. Lyon has brought before me but seven cases of breach of Contract, all of which have been compromised, the Ryots agreeing to fulfil their engagements, which would speak strongly in favor of the feelings existing between that Planter and his Ryots."

Mr. Yule, in the papers we publish, gives a very clear account of the cause of the outrage committed against Mr. Lyon. The Ryots in one factory of a *neighbouring* concern had been much oppressed by a Gomastah, and had not got redress from the manager, nor from the magistrate or police. The deputy magistrate from Moorshedabad took no notice of their complaints and gave them no redress. They were irritated and encouraged to violence by his proceedings. "The oppressions they complained of were not enquired into, and the violence the result of these oppressions was unpunished :—

"The excitement spread among the Ryots of other Indigo concerns. They entered into a Dhurmgut or combination under religious sanction not to cultivate Indigo. They raised contributions to defray the costs which might be incurred by their refusal to cultivate. They established signals by the beating of drums to enable themselves to assemble quickly at any given spot. Darogahs, Jemadars and Burkundazes were sent to the Thannah where this was going on, but they were helpless. Large assemblies of Ryots took place at night on the drum signal being given, and sometimes even in the day time large bodies of men would assemble and proceed to this or that village on pretence of defending it from an attack by the factory. The police, however, reported constantly and in strong and urgent terms the state of affairs, plainly stating in a report of the 11th March, that a serious affray with murder would occur. Had any enquiry been instituted even then by a competent officer, matters would have been settled, but there was no officer in the sub-division, and no enquiry was made. More police were ordered out, but from the 14th March none of the police reports appear to have been noticed until the 26th idem. The Ryots got worse and worse, the infection spread to the villages of Mr. Lyon's Beniagram factory above five miles from Ancoro, on the 19th drums were then heard by night answering each other from the villages all round."

After this followed the attack upon Mr. Lyon's factory from which he was so providentially saved. Mr. Yule has condemned the Ryots to imprisonment, but he thus speaks of them :—-

" Those unfortunate wretches whom I have just convicted and sentenced, those who were killed and wounded, many who have fled the country were led into the guilt for which they have suffered by the conduct of the deputy magistrate sent to enquire into the Ancora case, by the subsequent absence of an officer from the sub-division, and by the neglect with which the police reports were treated."

The cause of the outrage was not the Planter's oppression but the conduct of the deputy magistrate, who was perhaps as good a man as either Mr. Herschell or Mr. Eden, and who if examined before a Commission, would have probably given evidence against the character of the Messrs. Lyon, because their factories " had been the scene of the gravest outbreaks on the part of the Ryots that he had seen in any district." That Mr. Herschell's own conduct was the cause of the outbreaks he witnessed is very probable from the fact, that while he was in that district hs was severely rebuked by the Judge for passing most unjust orders in consequence of his ignorance of the vernacular, all of which was most fully set forth in the columns of the *Dacca News* some two or three years ago.

In conclusion, we shall quote what Mr. Yule says with regard to the cause of the poor Ryots having been betrayed into such an outrage against the law, and his opinion with regard to Mr. Lyon's gallant conduct and its result :—

" The reports show how the Ryots, at first amenable to remonstrances from the police, gradually learnt to disregard them till they attacked Beniagram in open daylight, and in

defiance of a considerable police force present on the spot.
The Ryots appeared to have said all along that what they
wanted was a Hakim to enquire into their grievances, and the
prisoners in this case plainly told me that they never would
have been in the scrape they were, had a Hakim been at hand.
I say the same, and this belief renders the duty of passing
sentence, at all times a painful one, infinitely more so in this
case than usual.

"In conclusion, I must observe that Mr. Lyon by his determined defence saved not only his own life and property, but
had the attack on Beniagram been successful, every Planter
and factory in this sub-division and Maldah would, I verily
believe, have been attacked, and there is no saying how far the
outbreak might have spread. Mr. Lyon had quelled the spirit
of destruction before almost it was known to be abroad."

We trust that Mr. Grant will now acknowledge that his
magistrates and police, and Government are not all faultless,
and that the country may owe something even to a despised
Planter.—*Ibid., December* 7.

(From the " Calcutta Englishman" of the 8th December, 1860).

The secret of the long-continued neglect of Government
securities with increasing bank balances, and money lying everywhere idle, is to be found in petitions such as that given below,
presented this morning to the Legislative Council from all the
leading mercantile men, and many native capitalists. It is to
be found also in the universal remonstrance against the Govern-
mental support of Mr. Grant and his policy, despite their own
recognition of the difficulties every day accumulating around the
position to which his determined enmity to Mofussil interlopers
upon the Civil Service district autocracies has brought them.
The resistance to the Planter, and repudiation of every contract
with him, in which Mr. Grant has tutored and supported the
Ryot, has developed itself into the destruction of interloping
property, and resistance to rent-paying as well as contracts,
and that in districts where no complaint has ever lain against
the Anglo-Indian residents, who bid fair to be involved in the
common ruin which is completing the long-foreseen result of
Mr. Grant's "success." All the circulars that the victorious
Bengal Government can write will be of no avail with the
Ryots who see that he is still in power. They continue to
read or listen to his circulars and proclamations only in the
sense in which he first taught them to interpret them, and they

treat as lies and cunning snares anything which implies that any change of sentiment or policy can weaken the *intente cordiale* which unites the "small capitalists" of Bengal and their great patron in their common enmity to the Planter. The weight of the English press has made itself felt most terribly in the ranks of the old aristocracy, who begin to think that there may be something in what every non-official in India has been telling them all along, when they see those sentiments, even more strongly expressed, and the self-same arguments carried to even harsher conclusions by the whole leading press of England. We told our friends and readers in England long before, what would be the drift and the worth of the report of the Indigo Commission; we told them long ago that the resistance of the Ryots would not long be confined to Indigo Contracts, and we tell them now what the Government know, but would fain discredit, that the policy of the Bengal Government has brought Bengal to that point at which any accident at any hour, may rouse large districts from their condition of passive resistance to payments, into an active *jacquerie* only to be put down, by force of arms, at which the very loudest in protest would be the men whose folly brought about the mischief. Meanwhile, Mr. Grant has the satisfaction of seeing the men who, on his assuming his lieutenancy, were men of wealth, improving whole districts and opening up the path of civilization, now seeking employment in which their energies may make fresh fortunes, not, we may hope to be at the mercy of such Governments as that of Bengal under Mr. Grant.

www.ingramcontent.com/pod-product-compliance
Lightning Source LLC
Chambersburg PA
CBHW031057280326
41928CB00049B/893